LEYENDAS
LEGENDS

To my dad, Jorge Raul Mancillas,
a legend in his own right. —MM

To my Brazilian, Peruvian, and Colombian family,
I'm a happy consequence of your extraordinary lives. —IZ

Text copyright © 2025 by Mónica Mancillas.
Illustrations copyright © 2025 by Isadora Zeferino.
All rights reserved. No part of this book may be reproduced in any form without written permission from the publisher.

Library of Congress Cataloging-in-Publication Data available.

ISBN 978-1-7972-1198-5

Manufactured in China.

Design by Jill Turney.
Typeset in Artegra Sans Condensed, P22Posada, HWT Artz, and YWFT Ultramagnetic.
The illustrations in this book were rendered digitally.

10 9 8 7 6 5 4 3 2 1

Chronicle books and gifts are available at special quantity discounts to corporations, professional associations, literacy programs, and other organizations. For details and discount information, please contact our premiums department at corporategifts@chroniclebooks.com or at 1-800-759-0190.

Chronicle Books LLC
680 Second Street
San Francisco, California 94107

Chronicle Books—we see things differently.
Become part of our community at www.chroniclekids.com.

LEYENDAS
LEGENDS

60 LATINE PEOPLE WHO CHANGED THE WORLD

By Mónica Mancillas

Illustrated by Isadora Zeferino

CHRONICLE BOOKS
SAN FRANCISCO

CONTENTS

Introduction 3
Celia Cruz, Singer 4
Matilde Hidalgo, Physician, Poet, and Activist 6
Antônio Carlos Jobim, Composer 8
Eva Perón (Evita), Actor and First Lady of Argentina 10
Pura Belpré, Writer and Librarian 12
Lucila Godoy Alcagaya (Gabriela Mistral), Poet and Teacher 14
José Castellanos Contreras, Diplomat and War Hero 16
Wifredo Lam, Artist 18
Amalia Hernández, Dancer and Choreographer 20
Frida Kahlo, Artist 22
Violeta Parra, Singer, Composer, and Artist 24
Ildaura Murillo-Rohde, Nurse 26
Tito Puente, Musician and Composer 28
Gabriel García Márquez, Writer 30
César Milstein, Biochemist 32
Dolores Huerta, Labor Organizer and Activist 34
Jaime Escalante, Public School Teacher 36
Rita Moreno, Actor, Singer, and Dancer 38
Walter Mercado, Astrologer and TV Personality 40
Roberto Clemente, Baseball Player 42
Sylvia Mendez, Activist 44
Florentina López de Jesús, Artisan and Activist 46
Maria Bueno, Tennis Player 48
Joan Baez, Singer and Activist 50
Edson Arantes do Nascimento (Pelé), Footballer/Soccer Player 52
Mario J. Molina, Chemist 54
Susana Baca, Singer and Songwriter 56
Reverend Gérard Jean-Juste, Human Rights Activist 58
Paulo Coelho, Lyricist and Novelist 60
Franklin Chang-Díaz, Astronaut and Physicist 62
Sylvia Rivera, Gay Liberation and Transgender Rights Activist 64

Sonia Sotomayor, Supreme Court Justice 66
María Elena Salinas, Journalist and News Anchor 68
Maricel Presilla, Chef, Writer, and Historian 70
Sandra Cisneros, Writer 72
Mari Carmen Ramírez, Museum Curator 74
Ellen Ochoa, Astronaut 76
Rigoberta Menchú Tum, Activist 78
Isabel Toledo, Fashion Designer 80
Jean-Michel Basquiat, Artist 82
Mónica Ponce de León, Architect 84
Máxima Acuña de Chaupe, Activist 86
Sylvia Poll, Swimmer 88
Berta Cáceres, Activist 90
Shakira, Singer and Songwriter 92
Abuelas de Plaza de Mayo, Activists 94
Luis von Ahn, Computer Scientist and Entrepreneur 96
Victor Pineda, Disability Activist 98
Ruben Vives, Journalist 100
Carolina Contreras, Hair Stylist, Blogger, and Activist 102
Wit López, Artist 104
Jillian Mercado, Model and Activist 106
Elizabeth Acevedo, Writer and Poet 108
Dior Vargas, Activist 110
Alexandria Ocasio-Cortez, Activist and Politician 112
Yalitza Aparicio, Actor and Activist 114
Indya Moore, Actor, Model, and Activist 116
Jamie Margolin, Climate Justice Activist 118
Jharrel Jerome, Actor 120
Sophie Cruz, Activist 122
Selected Bibliography 124
About the Author 130
About the Illustrator 130

INTRODUCTION

When I was a child, I was often told by my peers that I didn't "look Mexican." They knew I was *something* other than white, but they couldn't put their finger on exactly what. My green eyes and auburn hair didn't align with the images they had been fed by American television of Mexican people. In their minds, Mexicans—in fact, *all* Latin American people—were dark-skinned with black hair and brown eyes.

But it wasn't just my physical appearance that challenged what my friends had been taught to believe about people from Latin America. I was studious, smart, and ambitious, and I had dreams of becoming a scientist, an opera singer, a college student. What they had been told was that Latin Americans were "lazy," "job-stealing," and, often, "criminals." So, how could it be that my family and I were so different from what they'd seen on TV?

The truth is, at one point, even *I* wasn't sure if I was "Mexican" in the truest sense. Though I was born in Mexico and had a Latin American family, I didn't always feel like I fit in. I struggled to speak Spanish fluently and was, in many ways, culturally American. But my name was Mancillas. I held a Mexican passport. And I loved the place where I was born.

It wasn't until I brought this sense of confusion to my father that things started to change. When I shared my worry that I wasn't "Mexican" enough, he told me "Mexican" wasn't just one thing. He took me on my first extensive trip through Mexico, introducing me to the diverse cuisines, cultures, and topography. I saw jungles, beaches, pyramids, museums, and people of all ethnicities and backgrounds. It was the first time I was exposed to the idea that Latin American people can truly be *anything*—that the stereotypes I had been fed throughout my life weren't only harmful but completely untrue.

It was with that spirit that I decided to write this book—to take readers on that same journey so they might be freed of the biased representations of an uninformed society. Because the truth is that "Latin American" looks like *many* things, and there is no right or wrong way to be one. We are Black, white, and every shade in between. We come from all different backgrounds. There is *nothing* we cannot do if we just believe we are capable. The extraordinary people whose lives are chronicled in this book are evidence of this very principle. I hope you are as inspired by reading their amazing stories as I was when writing them.

CELIA CRUZ

Singer
1925–2003
Heritage: Cuban

CELIA CRUZ was born to sing. She was a naturally gifted performer, possessing a musical talent that her mother recognized from a young age. As a child, Celia sang her siblings to sleep at her mother's request. And when she was a teen, she sang in a radio talent contest called Tea Time—and won!

Although her father pushed her to pursue a more traditional career, Celia's mother encouraged her to keep performing.

She won several more radio contests while singing in live cabarets, enchanting her audiences with her powerful voice and charismatic onstage personality.

It was clear to Celia that she had a future as a singer, but her father disagreed. At his urging, she reluctantly enrolled in the National Teacher's College and began studying to become a teacher.

Though Celia wanted to appease her father, she could not abandon her calling. She continued to perform, encouraged by the appreciation of her growing audience. Seeking to find a compromise with her father, she transferred to a college of music—but she was soon urged by one of her professors to drop out and pursue singing full time.

In 1948, Celia joined a troupe of dancers and singers called Las Mulatas de Fuego—her first big step toward a career as a singer!

Two years later, she replaced the lead singer of Cuba's most famous orchestra, La Sonora Matancera, with whom she toured for many years and recorded several albums. While Celia was on tour in Mexico, Cuba underwent an armed revolution against a corrupt and tyrannical government. Instead of returning to her war-ravaged homeland, in 1961, Celia decided to settle in the United States—a move that infuriated Fidel Castro. Perceiving the move as a slight against his new regime, he banned Celia from ever returning home to Cuba. Though deeply painful, this forced exile would change the course of her life and career forever.

After moving to New York and marrying the orchestra's trumpet player, Pedro Knight, Celia decided to embark on a solo career. She began working with legendary musician Tito Puente, with whom she went on to record several albums. Performing with Tito gave Celia a bigger reach than she ever had before—and her extravagant costumes and winning stage persona helped Tito's band grow its audience even further.

Together, Tito and Celia helped usher in a brand-new era of Latin music, fusing elements of Afro-Cuban rhythms with American influences to create a new genre called *salsa*.

Salsa was an exciting new form of high-energy music and dance that had nightclubs across the nation on fire—the pulsating thrum of the clave beat pulling everyone to the dance floor.

In 1974, Celia signed with the Latin record label Vaya, which helped her become known as the Queen of Salsa. Celia recorded countless cherished songs, including the classic dance hit "Quimbara," breaking barriers in the male-dominated world of music and unapologetically celebrating her Afro-Latinidad.

Celia recorded more than eighty albums during her sixty-year career, twenty-three of which were certified gold (including *Celia & Johnny*, featuring Johnny Pacheco).

She won three Grammys and four Latin Grammys and was nominated for several others. At the height of her career, she even earned an entry in the *Guinness Book of World Records* when she performed at a free outdoor concert for a crowd of 250,000 people!

Celia made an indelible impact on the music world that lives on today: in the schools and parks that bear her name, in the books and documentaries that chronicle her life, and in the many songs that stand as a testament to her timeless talent. Her iconic look and unmistakable voice changed the landscape of Latin music forever, bringing a popularity to salsa music that has endured.

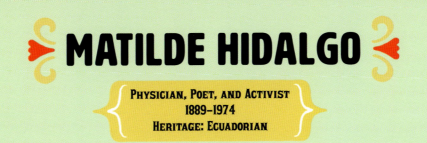

MATILDE HIDALGO

Physician, Poet, and Activist
1889–1974
Heritage: Ecuadorian

As a child, **MATILDE HIDALGO** loved to learn—school was her greatest pleasure! She dreamed that someday, when she grew up, she would become a doctor. But the world that Matilde was born into did not encourage such ambitions in girls. In Ecuador, girls stopped going to school when they were only eleven.

> Matilde wanted to continue studying and believed girls deserved the same education and opportunities as boys.

Her older brother, Antonio, agreed. Antonio spoke with the director of an all-boys high school—Colegio Bernardo Valdivieso in Loja, Ecuador—and asked them to enroll Matilde. At first, she received no response. But one month later, she finally got an answer: Matilde was going to school!

At first, Matilde was overjoyed! But her victory came at a stunning cost. With the exception of her mother and brother, Matilde was shunned by her own friends and family, and even her church. She was no longer allowed to attend Mass but, instead, had to stand outside the church and listen from the front steps.

> Women in her neighborhood told their daughters to stay away from Matilde, afraid she was setting a bad example.

After all, girls were not supposed to spend their days at school learning to be doctors! Girls were supposed to stay home and raise families. But Matilde had other plans for her life.

Although hurt by the rejection of her friends and community, Matilde persevered and stayed on her path. In 1913, she became the first woman in Ecuador's history to graduate from high school. But she wasn't done yet! Matilde was still determined to pursue her dream of being a doctor. When the local college refused to let her enroll, she applied elsewhere and was finally accepted at the University of Cuenca in Azuay. She became the first woman in Ecuador to earn a bachelor's degree and went on to earn a doctorate in medicine.

> In 1921, Matilde became the first female doctor in Ecuador's history.

Despite achieving this tremendous goal, Matilde was still troubled by all the unspoken rules that prevented women from being treated as equals in their own country. She believed strongly that women had the right to contribute to society and help make the rules. To do that, the women of Ecuador needed the right to vote.

In 1924, Matilde tried to register to vote on election day, but her request was denied. Everyone said women couldn't vote! But Matilde pointed out that there was nothing in the Ecuadorian constitution that prevented her from voting—the only requirements in the Ecuadorian constitution pertained to citizenship, age, and literacy. She was a citizen, she was the right age, and she could read. There was nothing in the constitution saying she had to be a man to vote. She took her case to parliament and the National Electoral Council, which eventually conceded.

> Matilde became the first woman in all of Latin America to vote in a national election.

That was only the beginning. In 1929, inspired by Matilde's actions, Ecuador approved women's suffrage and became the first country in Latin America to allow *all* women to vote in national elections! But why stop there? With so many barriers still needing to be broken, Matilde decided she would become the first woman to run for public office. In doing so, she became the first female elected public official in her hometown of Loja, the first local councilwoman, and, eventually, the first female vice president of Machala's city council.

> Matilde's tenacity and refusal to accept traditional gender expectations led her to break through every systemic barrier that kept women from advancing as equals in their own country.

Because of Matilde, women could now study, build careers, vote, and run for public office. Her courage and determination changed the course of history for women not only in Ecuador but also throughout Latin America.

ANTÔNIO CARLOS JOBIM

Composer
1927–1994
Heritage: Brazilian

ANTÔNIO CARLOS JOBIM grew up in the tropics of Brazil, where the starry nights and seaside breezes felt to him like a song just waiting to be written. The streets of Ipanema, where he lived, swayed with samba rhythms. And at home, his uncles' guitars filled the house with dulcet melodies.

Antônio loved tinkering with the piano at the primary school his mother ran, but it wasn't until he turned fourteen that he began studying music in earnest.

Upon noticing Antônio's musical inclinations, his stepfather enrolled him in piano lessons with a highly reputed composer who taught him the fundamentals of music theory. After finishing his secondary studies, Antônio briefly considered becoming an architect. But the unwritten song still called to him. He decided to try his hand at becoming a full-time musician.

Antônio began his musical journey on the Rio de Janeiro nightclub circuit, performing in small clubs called *inferninhos* (little infernos). He soon moved on from covering songs to performing original compositions, supplementing his income by transcribing and arranging music for local recording artists.

And then Antônio's first big break came.

Odeon Records—one of Brazil's largest record labels—offered him the esteemed position of musical director!

This new role offered Antônio the unparalleled opportunity to connect with other world-class artists, and in 1958, he began a life-changing collaboration with singer-guitarist João Gilberto. Together, they released a groundbreaking single called "Chega de Saudade" ("No More Blues"). Though the song was only mildly received, the duo's album bearing the same name made waves.

It was the first time anyone had heard anything like it—this sultry twist on Brazilian samba known as *bossa nova*.

The blend of Gilberto's acoustic melodies with Antônio's intimate harmonies enchanted audiences all over the world, inspiring a new movement within Latin music.

The following year, Antônio helped score the music for a film called *Orfeu Negro* (*Black Orfeus*), which won the Academy Award for Best Foreign Film and earned Antônio international recognition.

By the early 1960s, everyone knew the gentle rhythms of bossa nova—that signature sound that combined cool jazz with Brazilian samba.

Antônio's songs were covered by musical greats such as Frank Sinatra and Ella Fitzgerald, going on to become standards in the musical canon for many years to come.

Antônio composed more than four hundred songs during his decades-long career, including chart toppers such as "The Girl from Ipanema," "Desafinado," and "One Note Samba." In 1991, he was inducted into the Songwriters Hall of Fame for the profound influence he exerted on the landscape of twentieth-century music. Antônio's trailblazing compositions brought Brazilian rhythms into the musical spotlight, inspiring songwriters and performers around the world with the tropical sway of bossa nova. He brought the starry nights and seaside breezes of his childhood Brazil into the hearts of adoring fans all over the globe.

EVA PERÓN (EVITA)

{ Actor and First Lady of Argentina
1919–1952
Heritage: Argentinean }

EVA PERÓN—or **EVITA**, as she would later become known—dedicated her life to helping the working-class people of Argentina. The youngest of five children, Evita grew up in poverty in the Argentine Pampas after a drastic shift in political power left her father in financial straits. Her father wasn't married to her mother, and he had a wife and second family to support. Because of this, when he died, Evita and her family were left to struggle on their own.

Despite her family's financial hardships, Evita found solace in simple childhood games. Like other children, she liked to climb trees and play hopscotch and hide-and-seek.

> **She especially loved reciting poetry, feeling strongly from a young age that she had something to say.**

Whenever she could, Evita displayed her talent over the loudspeaker for the whole town to hear.

When Evita was fifteen, she left her small town and moved to the city of Buenos Aires, following her dream of becoming an actress. Despite her lack of experience or training, Evita was soon using her gifts on stage, in film, and in radio productions. In 1937, she took her first movie role in a film called ¡Segundos Afuera! (Seconds Out!)—and soon after, she signed a contract to perform on one of the largest radio stations in the city!

> **Though her wealth and celebrity grew over the years, Evita never forgot her humble background.**

In 1944, she volunteered to help victims of the devastating San Juan earthquake and met Juan Perón, a rising star in the Argentine government, in the process. Juan's public criticism of conservative politics eventually led to his arrest. Evita—a powerful force in her own right—helped organize a mass demonstration that led to his release, and the two were married shortly after. In 1945, the Labor Party asked Juan to run for president, and Evita made Argentinean history as the first woman to campaign by her husband's side! She was vital in helping Juan get elected to the presidency.

> **She never missed a chance to speak directly to the people and became beloved all over Argentina.**

A strong believer in women's rights, Evita played a central role in her husband's government. She served unofficially as the minister of health and labor, and she spent her days visiting hospitals, factories, and orphanages while working to improve conditions for the working class through higher wages, social welfare benefits, and improved health policy. She even coerced her adversaries—the social elite whose interests went counter to her policies—into contributing funds to her foundation, which provided money, food, and medicine to those in need.

> **Thanks to Evita's efforts, in 1947, Argentina passed women's suffrage, and women in Argentina voted for the first time in 1951.**

That same year, Evita was nominated for vice president, running on the same ticket as her husband, but her declining health and opposition from the military forced her to turn down the opportunity.

In 1952, Juan Perón began his second term as Argentina's president. But tragically, Evita died from cancer within a month of his inauguration, at the age of thirty-three. The streets filled with grieving mourners, some of whom urged the Catholic Church to declare Evita a saint in recognition of her many good works.

> **She remains an icon throughout the world to this day.**

Her formidable charm and spirit were a beacon of hope for the working-class people of Argentina, for whom she fought her whole life without compromise.

PURA BELPRÉ

{ Writer and Librarian
1899–1982
Heritage: Puerto Rican }

PURA BELPRÉ grew up listening to her grandmother tell stories that had been passed through their family for generations: the whimsical, culturally layered folktales of her native Puerto Rico. Stories like "Pérez and Martina" (a tragic romance between a mouse and a cockroach) formed the backdrop of Pura's childhood and shaped her sense of identity.

From a very young age, she knew she wanted to share the tales she loved while growing up.

So, in 1919, she enrolled at the University of Puerto Rico with plans to become a teacher.

But everything changed when Pura was given the chance to visit New York City. Though the stay was meant to be temporary, she could not bring herself to leave. Pulled back to her love of stories, she was hired as a "Hispanic assistant" to the growing population of Spanish speakers visiting the 135th Street branch of the New York Public Library in Harlem, becoming the first Puerto Rican employee in its history!

Pura was soon put to work reshelving and organizing books in the adult and children's rooms.

She found so much joy in sharing stories with others that she quickly decided to become a librarian.

Pura enrolled at the Library School of the New York Public Library, where she took a class on storytelling. Inspired by her childhood, she wrote a retelling of "Pérez and Martina" as a class assignment. Then she had an idea: Why not share it at a special story hour for children? The tale met with such a positive response that Pura decided to institute bilingual story hours, traveling to branches throughout the city to encourage Spanish-speaking children to come to the library.

Pura's story times were magical experiences for adults and children alike. She often used handmade puppets to bring her stories to life. She lit cozy candles, which the children blew out with a wish when story time was over. To bridge the divide between the library and its patrons, she added books in Spanish to the library's collection and held cultural events to celebrate Latine holiday traditions. She also attended meetings of civic organizations, such as the Puerto Rican Brotherhood and La Liga Puertorriqueña e Hispana, in an effort to bring more Spanish-speaking patrons to the library. Pura did what no librarian before her had ever thought to do.

For the first time, Latine children and their families felt like they, too, were truly welcome at the New York Public Library.

During Pura's forty-plus-year tenure as a New York Public Library librarian, she completely transformed the libraries of Harlem. She worked to expand community outreach, giving much-needed visibility to a growing population that had once been entirely overlooked.

And she even enriched the literary canon with stories of her own!

Pérez y Martina, Pura's retelling of her favorite folktale, was published in 1932, making history as the first Spanish-language book to be released by a major US publisher. And Pura didn't stop there—she went on to write many more books based on the beloved stories of her childhood. Throughout her life, she worked tirelessly to collect, preserve, and publish Puerto Rican folklore.

Through Pura's efforts, the Harlem libraries became hubs of Latine culture, providing models of inclusion for libraries and communities across the United States. Her legacy is recognized every year with the American Library Association's presentation of the Pura Belpré Award, which honors Latine authors and illustrators for creating children's literature that portrays, affirms, and celebrates Latine cultural experiences. Because of Pura, libraries across the United States now offer bilingual story hours as part of their regular programming—and, increasingly, the children's sections are filled with more and more stories that represent the cultures of *all* readers.

LUCILA GODOY ALCAGAYA
(GABRIELA MISTRAL)

{ Poet and Teacher
1889–1957
Heritage: Chilean }

LUCILA GODOY ALCAGAYA—or **GABRIELA MISTRAL**, as she would later be known—was born with the heart of a poet.

> Though her family was poor, her upbringing in the Andean village of Monte Grande was rich with poetry.

Gabriela's abuela encouraged her to read and memorize biblical poems, and her father loved to write poems and sing to her as he played the guitar. He left the family when she was three years old, but he came back occasionally for visits, and their time together inspired Gabriela's growing sense of creativity. She began writing and publishing her work in local publications when she was just a teenager, using pseudonyms that reflected a feeling of isolation: Alguien (Someone), Alma (Soul), and Soledad (Loneliness).

This sense of loneliness took root when Gabriela left home at eleven to continue her education. She missed her family terribly. And the teachers at school did not always treat her fairly, accusing her of stealing, frowning on her writing, and calling her a troublemaker. She eventually dropped out of school, taking work as a teacher's aide to help her family survive.

> Life was hard, but Gabriela found glimmers of hope in the darkness.

When she was seventeen, she fell in love with a railway worker named Romelio. The relationship was a welcome but brief respite from her profound loneliness—it came to a tragic end when Romelio took his own life. Gabriela poured her anguish into her poetry, writing pieces like "Dolor" ("Pain"), which detailed the heartbreak of her first great love.

Gabriela spent the next many years teaching throughout the country and becoming even more profoundly connected to the struggles of Chile's most vulnerable populations. As a teacher, she witnessed the challenges faced by Indigenous and working-class families, prompting her to advocate for women, children, and those communities left without a voice.

> She channeled these experiences into writing, weaving fragments of her sorrows, her compassion, and her faith into deeply emotional poems.

In 1914, Gabriela won first place in a national literary contest for *Los Sonetos de la Muerte* (*The Sonnets of the Dead*)—poems about the many losses she had suffered in the early part of her life.

In 1922, Gabriela published her first book, *Desolación* (*Desolation*), and began lecturing in other countries. That same year, she accepted an invitation from the Mexican government to help reform its education system. Gabriela nurtured her literary career as she continued her travels, teaching Spanish literature at universities throughout the United States and serving as a Chilean consul in Naples, Lisbon, and Madrid. She also published many more books, each infused with her life experiences.

Twenty-three years after the publication of *Desolación*, Gabriela was honored as the first Latin American Nobel Laureate in Literature—and just a few years after that, she received the Chilean National Prize for Literature! In spite of the many pains she had suffered, Gabriela rose to great acclaim, channeling her suffering into education and becoming a light of hope for her country. Today, her poetry is a staple in the curricula of schools all over Chile, where she is remembered for her immeasurable talents and lifelong advocacy.

JOSÉ CASTELLANOS CONTRERAS

> Diplomat and War Hero
> 1893–1977
> Heritage: Salvadoran

All throughout his life, **JOSÉ CASTELLANOS CONTRERAS** was unafraid of doing what was right. Though he was born to a wealthy, conservative family, he was troubled by the plight of the poor, the subjugation of Indigenous peoples, and the inequalities routinely endured by women. Like his father before him, José did as his family expected and rose through the ranks of the army.

But he still could not help speaking out against the injustices he saw all around him.

In 1937, just before the onset of World War II, José's open criticism of the government landed him in exile—he was sent to Europe to serve as a diplomat.

José was first posted to England, then reassigned to Germany, where he witnessed firsthand the grave mistreatment of Jews by the Nazi regime. In 1938, Nazi troops took to the streets of Germany, destroying homes, businesses, and lives on what would become known as Kristallnacht—the Night of Broken Glass. On this night, more than thirty thousand Jewish men were forcibly arrested and sent to concentration camps. Thousands of synagogues and Jewish businesses were destroyed. Countless Jewish citizens were beaten and killed. And this was only the beginning of the Nazis' plan to exterminate *all* Jewish people.

José was horrified. Desperate to help however he could, he appealed to the Salvadoran government for permission to grant visas to Jewish citizens fleeing Germany. But El Salvador, like the United States and Britain, did not want any trouble with Germany. José's appeal was denied, and he was transferred to the war-neutral country of Switzerland. But he was not deterred so easily.

Forced to choose between his orders and what he believed to be right, José decided to take matters into his own hands.

José began fighting back by forging citizenship papers for his friend György Mandl, a Transylvanian Jew whose family was facing deportation from Switzerland. He changed György's name to George Mandel-Mantello and appointed him to a nonexistent diplomatic position—an act that was both dangerous and illegal but that would save the lives of György and his family. But saving just one family was not enough. There were too many lives at stake! To maximize their impact, José and György set up a factory and printed falsified papers that granted Salvadoran citizenship to thousands of Jews all over Eastern Europe.

Together, they saved the lives of an estimated forty thousand people—people whose descendants now reside in countries all over the world.

After the war, José lived out his days in obscurity in El Salvador, never seeking recognition for doing what he believed to be right. It wasn't until 2010 that he was posthumously recognized by Yad Vashem—Israel's official memorial to victims of the Holocaust—as one of the Righteous among the Nations. Through his courageous interventions, José showed the world that *true* bravery is refusing to back down in the face of grave injustice.

WIFREDO LAM

{ Artist
1902–1982
Heritage: Cuban }

WIFREDO LAM was born to a newly independent Cuba, his own legacy a map of the complex history of the country. His father was Chinese and his mother part Spanish, part African, so he inherited the history of both colonizer and the enslaved.

His family's beliefs were a cultural amalgam of Catholic and West African Yoruba traditions, and his upbringing bore the marks of a nation still grappling with the idea of liberation.

Though Wifredo's homeland was finally free from the horrors of slavery, the effects of oppression lingered in a deeply stratified country. This context shaped his childhood and, eventually, his art, which would come to reflect his fascination with both Western and African traditions.

Wifredo's artistic passions were ignited when he was just fourteen, after his family moved to Havana. He spent hours in the city's sprawling botanical gardens, trying to capture the beauty of its tropical flora. As a young adult, he abandoned his studies in law to enroll at the Professional School of Arts in Havana.

Soon after, Wifredo exhibited his work at the Salón de Bellas Artes—where his talent won him a scholarship that enabled him to move to Madrid!

There, he studied the work of great Spanish artists such as Diego Velázquez and Francisco Goya, along with that of sixteenth-century artists such as Hieronymus Bosch and Bruegel the Elder. Wifredo was consistently surprised by the similarities he found between Western art and so-called primitive art—the creative work of his African ancestors, which the world still saw as inferior.

Wifredo lived in Spain for fourteen years. He married and started a family there—but his joy was cut short when his wife and child died of tuberculosis.

> **Anguished and alone, Wifredo sought comfort from friends with whom he shared anti-fascist sympathies.**

He aided in the fight against Spanish dictator Francisco Franco, designing posters and working in a munitions factory. At the same time, Wifredo poured his suffering into his art, creating countless paintings that featured mother and child. In 1938, he left Spain for Paris, hoping to make a fresh start.

In Paris, Wifredo found new life among the city's avant-garde, which enthusiastically embraced him—including painter Pablo Picasso, with whom he shared a love of African art forms. Wifredo's work was highly influenced by his new set of surrealist friends.

> **In 1939, he had his first solo exhibition, with another to follow (alongside Pablo!) in New York.**

Though Wifredo's name was finally gaining traction, his life was soon upended once again, as he was forced to flee to the Caribbean to escape German forces during World War II. He sheltered with friends and fellow painters, feverishly creating new works, among them the animalistic hybrid portraits that would become his signature style.

In 1941, Wifredo finally returned to his homeland, where he was dismayed to find that, in the twenty years he had been abroad, not much had changed. As in his childhood, Cuba was still deeply entrenched in the mire of colonial oppression, struggling to free itself of the societal stratification that resulted from hundreds of years of slavery. Wifredo began immersing himself in African traditions, which, coupled with his reflections on the state of the country, inspired an explosion of new artwork.

> **He painted more than one hundred canvases in his first year back home, among them *La Jungla* (*The Jungle*), one of his most influential and renowned works.**

La Jungla combined elements of Afro-Cuban mysticism with modern cubist art, examining Cuba's violent history of oppression through animalistic figures in a sugarcane field. These vivid images scandalized conservative crowds in New York, cementing Wifredo's international reputation as a revolutionary twentieth-century artist.

Over the following three decades, Wifredo's art continued to evolve, combining cubist elements with African influences to create a distinct style that was altogether new. His paintings expressed the fusion of culture that had defined his childhood in Cuba while also challenging the systems of oppression that relegated Afro-Cubans to the margins. Wifredo became one of the most influential painters in Latin American history, renowned along with cultural icons such as Frida Kahlo and Diego Rivera. His work inspired artists all over the world, and many remain captivated by his unique style and powerful message.

AMALIA HERNÁNDEZ

{ Dancer and Choreographer
1917–2000
Heritage: Mexican }

AMALIA HERNÁNDEZ was born during the renaissance that emerged from the Mexican Revolution, when the notion of what it meant to be Mexican was rapidly evolving. During the Revolution, the people of Mexico rose up against colonizing powers after centuries of oppression, and in the years that followed, Mexican artists were called on to help shape the country's newly emerging national identity.

It was during this cultural awakening that Amalia first fell in love with dance.

She was mesmerized by the beautiful and elegant dancers she had seen at the circus, and she wanted to move gracefully just like them.

She dreamed that maybe, one day, she could even perform at Mexico's new national theater, the Palacio de Bellas Artes! Amalia's parents encouraged her love of the arts, using their wealth to build a private studio where she and her sisters could learn to dance from a world-renowned teacher. And when it became clear that Amalia was set on becoming a professional dancer, her father sent her to San Antonio, Texas, where she learned ballet.

But Amalia was not satisfied with studying only classical dance. She was deeply drawn to the popular and Indigenous dances she had seen during her family's travels—the traditional folk dances of San Luis Potosí, Jalisco, and Veracruz, some dating all the way back to Mexico's precolonial history.

Amalia loved her Mexican heritage. She wanted to learn *these* dances—the dances of her country—too!

Determined to learn as much as she could about Mexican dance, Amalia began studying with Waldeen, a well-respected choreographer of modern dance who also loved Mexican arts and culture. Amalia turned her focus to adapting Mexico's traditional dances for the theater. Working closely with historians and anthropologists, she developed choreography that interpreted the dances of more than sixty different regions of Mexico.

This revolutionary new form painted a picture of the rich and dynamic cultural traditions of her country, becoming known as *baile folklórico*.

It was not long before Amalia founded her own company of dancers, the Ballet Folklórico de Mexico, which debuted on national television and was soon touring internationally. The Ballet Folklórico captivated the world with its vibrant costumes, set design, and choreography. The company soon became an important cultural symbol of Mexico and was invited to take up permanent residence in the Palacio de Bellas Artes—just as Amalia had dreamed!

Amalia went on to win hundreds of awards for her work as a choreographer, including the Prize of Nations in France and the National Prize of Culture in Mexico.

Her visionary work transformed the culture of dance across the globe, inspiring a new generation of dancers and showing the world just how rich and varied Mexican identity really is.

FRIDA KAHLO

Artist
1907–1954
Heritage: Mexican

FRIDA KAHLO was born in La Casa Azúl (the Blue House), in Mexico City, to an exacting Catholic mother and an adoring father. Though she was never formally trained as an artist, Frida was an observant child, always watching the world around her. Her father, a professional photographer, taught her all about the visual arts and how to retouch and color photographs. One of his friends also gave her drawing lessons.

These early influences would inform her life—a life lived with a creative passion despite many challenges.

When she was just six years old, Frida fell seriously ill with polio. She was bedridden for months, her damaged right leg and foot leaving her with a limp. Her father encouraged her to rehabilitate through exercise. So, defying gender norms for the first (but certainly *not* the last) time, Frida began boxing, wrestling, playing soccer, and participating in swim competitions. She would take this passionate refusal to conform into adolescence and beyond.

At age fifteen, Frida enrolled in a prestigious preparatory school, where she gravitated toward others like her who embraced self-expression. One of only a few girls admitted, she stood out further with her penchant for wearing traditional Mexican dresses with full skirts and handcrafted embroidery, her elaborate jewelry, and her big personality. She played pranks on her teachers and debated with her peers.

Frida identified as a "daughter of the Mexican Revolution" and believed in equality and freedom from oppression.

By age twenty, she had joined the Communist Party, where she hoped to promote meaningful social change.

Shortly after turning eighteen, tragedy struck: Frida was grievously injured in a terrible bus accident. She suffered several painful fractures, requiring a full body cast. Unable to attend school, Frida returned to the comforts of her childhood and began to paint about her suffering, creating the first of many self-portraits through which she would catalog her life experiences.

In 1928, Frida was reunited with an artist she'd first met at school, renowned muralist Diego Rivera.

Diego began visiting Frida regularly, offering to critique her paintings. The two fell in love quickly and were married the following year, drawn together by their political views and shared love of art. However, their swift romance soon spiraled into a stormy marriage, fraught with frequent arguments, separations, and, eventually, divorce.

Frida expressed her physical and emotional pain in a series of vibrant self-portraits, the first of which she sold shortly before her separation from Diego. The sale gave her a much-needed sense of financial independence and earned her an exhibition in New York City. The show was such a success that she became the first Mexican artist in the twentieth century to sell a painting to the prestigious Louvre Museum in Paris.

With her broken body and fractured heart on display for all the world, Frida truly became a celebrity in her own right.

Though her artistic life was thriving, Frida's health made it difficult to work. Still, she continued, and her paintings grew steadily in popularity. Then, in 1953, Frida was finally given her first solo exhibition in Mexico City—the same place where she had first learned to love the visual arts! Bedridden and in tremendous pain, Frida arrived at the Galería de Arte Contemporáneo by ambulance and spent the entire evening in her four-poster bed. *Nothing*—not even her failing health—would keep her from enjoying this hard-won moment.

A year later, Frida passed away at the age of forty-seven, leaving behind two hundred works of art and a legacy of political activism. Through all her trials, she never stopped campaigning for justice. Her art was a testament to a growing sense of national pride—a Mexican identity that revered Indigenous culture—as well as the fight for greater independence for women. Frida lived a life of tireless art making and activism in spite of profound personal struggles. She remains an icon around the world, ever remembered for her unique vision, the vulnerability expressed through her art, her unapologetic expression of her bisexuality, and her unbreakable spirit.

VIOLETA PARRA

{ Singer, Composer, and Artist
1917–1967
Heritage: Chilean }

For **VIOLETA PARRA** and her family, music was a lifeline—a way for them to combat the daily struggles of financial hardship. Though miserably poor, the family took great joy in performing together.

 Violeta's father was a music teacher who taught his children to play various instruments and traditional folk songs.

Violeta could sing and play the guitar, and she delighted in putting on shows for her friends, just like the circus performers who sometimes came to town. As her family traveled frequently to find work, music itself became a kind of home, a place of comfort that held them together.

But tragically, when Violeta was twelve years old, her father passed away. After his death, her brothers were forced to drop out of school, and all of their lives changed drastically. Violeta and her siblings had to figure out how to earn money for the family. Together, they used the skills their father had taught them to put food on the table. They began performing boleros, rancheras, and Mexican corridos in various nightclubs, ballrooms, and even circuses. Music—once a source of joy—became a means of surviving.

When her eldest brother, Nicanor, earned a scholarship to move to Santiago, Violeta's life changed again. He invited her along so she could study to become a teacher. She enrolled at the Normal School for Girls, but she quickly abandoned the program.

 Her heart belonged to music!

She and her sister Hilda began performing together as the Parra Sisters and made a decent living playing folk songs throughout the city.

In 1952, Violeta took her love of traditional folk songs on the road. She began traveling throughout rural Chile gathering the cuecas and tonados of ancient times that were slowly fading from collective memory. She interviewed folklorists, cataloging more than three thousand songs, folktales, and proverbs, and came to truly understand the social divisions existing in her country.

 Her own compositions took on a new tone, infused with a heavy folk influence and centering on themes of social justice and the challenges faced by marginalized people.

Violeta was openly critical of wealthy landowners who exploited the laboring classes, telling the stories of struggling Chileans through the powerful medium of song. She helped spark a musical movement known as *nueva canción*, a fusion of contemporary styles with traditional folk songs. She spent the next several years performing, recording, and teaching folklore before moving to Paris, where she quickly became an icon in the art world.

Violeta was more than a singer and composer—she was also a talented writer and visual artist. She sculpted, wrote poetry, and painted, often using art as a vehicle for political expression. In 1959 and 1960, she showed her work at the Chilean Feria de Artes Plásticas—the Fair of Plastic Arts. Four years later, she would become the first Latine creator to exhibit at the Louvre Museum in Paris!

 In 1966, Violeta wrote a song that would make her a musical legend for the ages.

"Gracias a la Vida" ("Thanks to Life") was a hit all over the world and has since been covered by musical greats like Mercedes Sosa, Joan Baez, and Michael Bublé.

While her artistic life flourished, Violeta's home life had begun to unravel in a series of personal tragedies—she suffered bouts of depression, the end of a love affair, and the death of a child. But through it all, music was a vital constant. Through song, she could express her pain.

Though Violeta tragically took her own life when she was only forty-nine, her legacy of art and song was instrumental in shaping music for future generations. Violeta brought new vitality to traditional art forms, displaying them to the world and altering the landscape of music forever. Her life wasn't easy, but she used her struggles to give others a voice through song, bringing about a rise of new musical forms while also preserving the folk music traditions that meant so much to her.

ILDAURA MURILLO-ROHDE

{ Nurse
1920–2010
Heritage: Panamanian }

Born to a family of health professionals, **ILDAURA MURILLO-ROHDE** grew up understanding the importance of quality health care. When World War II began, she felt compelled to use her passion for medicine to help the sick and injured. She served as a nurse throughout the war and then, in 1945, moved to the United States to begin her career in earnest.

Ildaura enrolled at the Medical and Surgical Hospital School of Nursing in San Antonio, Texas, where she earned her degree in 1948.

> **She was excited to learn and practice medicine, but she also felt isolated as one of very few Latine nurses in the United States.**

San Antonio was a city with a significant population of Latine residents. So why weren't there more Latine nurses serving the community? Ildaura decided this needed to change, and that change would begin with *her*.

Ildaura continued her studies in nursing at Columbia University, where she earned her bachelor's degree. Determined to become an academic who could address health policy at the highest levels, she then enrolled in New York University, where she earned her master's degree *and* became the college's first Latine nurse to earn a doctoral degree! She joined the faculty of the Nursing School at the State University of New York, where she quickly became a professor and eventually ascended all the way to dean. But the issue that Ildaura had first noticed as a nurse in San Antonio was the same everywhere she went:

> **There were too few Latine nurses in the workforce—and even fewer in academia.**

Ildaura decided to focus on changing the industry from the inside, beginning with the formation of a Spanish-speaking/Spanish-surname committee within the American Nurses Association. Though the association's stated mission was to advance and protect the needs of nurses throughout the United States, Ildaura felt that Latine communities were severely underserved.

> **The committee was not adequately addressing the dearth of Latine nurses—nor the unmet needs of a multilingual population with distinct cultural traditions and beliefs.**

She quickly discovered that a single committee was not enough to make formative changes. So, in 1976, Ildaura and fourteen other Latine nurses decided to address these deficiencies by forming their *own* organization: the National Association of Spanish-Speaking/Spanish-Surnamed Nurses. Four years later, the group changed its name to the National Association of Hispanic Nurses (NAHN)—and elected Ildaura as its first president! Ildaura worked hard to help the new institution grow, leading organizational efforts and even putting out the newsletter.

> **She aimed to advocate for both Latine nurses *and* the patients they served—and she was determined to provide educational and professional opportunities for those new to the industry.**

With the NAHN, Ildaura prioritized outreach to high school and college students, hoping to increase the number of Latine nurses in the workforce. She encouraged nurses to dream big and obtain doctoral degrees, maximizing their ability to inform public policies affecting their communities. Because of Ildaura's efforts, the NAHN grew from one to more than forty chapters, supporting the work of Latine nurses across the country!

In 1994, Ildaura was named a Living Legend by the American Nurses Association in honor of the many contributions she made to the nursing community throughout her lifetime. Her work to make the profession more accessible to people of Latine heritage continues to be recognized by the NAHN, which offers aspiring Latine nurses annual scholarships in Ildaura's name. Ildaura was one of the first Latine nurses in the United States to influence academic research and health policy—but thanks to her efforts, many more have followed in her footsteps. At last, her dream of seeing more Latine nurses in positions of leadership has come true.

TITO PUENTE

Musician and Composer
1923–2000
Heritage: Puerto Rican

TITO PUENTE was born amid the Latin rhythms of Spanish Harlem. His childhood was filled with the songs of his parents' native Puerto Rico: plaintive décimas, satirical plenas, and Afro-Cuban guarachas.

He loved to drum on pots and pans—so loudly, in fact, that the neighbors complained, begging his mother to enroll Tito in music lessons instead.

But lessons were difficult to afford. His father made very little and frequently lost money gambling. Tito's mother had to search her husband's pockets while he slept to pay for Tito's lessons.

But it was worth it. Tito was a natural, and he could not get enough music! He was captivated by the big swing bands, with their strong dance beats and electric energy, that were the soundtrack to World War II. When Tito was a kid, he saw drummer Gene Krupa in concert at the Paramount Theater and wanted to be just like him. When Gene drummed, all eyes were on him. His dynamic playing made the drums into a solo instrument in their own right. Tito had never seen that done before.

Maybe he could play like that, too!

When Tito was thirteen, he began playing timbales professionally and was eventually invited to join the popular band Machito and His Afro-Cubans. He gained valuable experience playing, performing, and rehearsing with Machito. But just like Machito's drummer before him, Tito was drafted to serve in World War II, where he became a bugler for the navy. He often performed on saxophone to entertain the crews and keep his skills fresh. One day, while aboard an aircraft carrier, Tito met jazz trumpeter Charlie Spivak. The two became fast friends, and Charlie's experience as a bandleader ignited Tito's interest in big band composition.

During his service in the navy, Tito served in nine battles and received a Presidential Commendation.

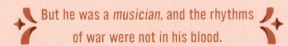

But he was a *musician*, and the rhythms of war were not in his blood.

When he returned home, Tito used the money he'd received from the GI Bill to enroll in the Juilliard School, a world-renowned university specializing in the arts. He studied composition, orchestration, and piano, but he soon became restless. The school's strict focus on classical music felt too confining to Tito. He decided it was time to form his *own* band—the Tito Puente Orchestra. Before long, his group was headlining alongside Machito and Tito Rodríguez at the Palladium Ballroom in New York City, where people came from all over to dance the night away.

Tito and his band drew crowds of dancers from all backgrounds and walks of life. Already mad with "mambo fever," audiences loved Tito's passionate solos. He soon became known as El Rey: the definitive "King" of Latin music. Tito's fusion of Latin rhythms with other popular genres captivated his audiences. He mixed elements of jazz, boogaloo, and salsa into his compositions, obscuring the boundaries of genre and helping popularize Afro-Cuban rhythms such as the cha-cha-chá. Tito recorded and released his first mambo album in 1950. Seven years later, his album *Dance Mania* topped the charts as a national bestseller. In 1970, the Latin rock star Carlos Santana covered one of Tito's best-known songs:

"Oye Como Va" became a hit all over the world!

Tito was tireless in his passion for music, playing two hundred to three hundred shows a year. During his career, he recorded more than one hundred albums and composed well over two hundred songs, winning five Grammy Awards and receiving the distinction of Living Legend from the Library of Congress in 2000. And Tito's legacy lives on in the rhythms we hear on the radio today! He shaped music, just as music shaped him, with his zeal for performing and composing. A true pioneer, he brought Latin sounds into mainstream music, drawing crowds to dance floors all over the world. Because of Tito, the rhythms of the Caribbean were now widely performed, celebrated, and beloved—the very same rhythms of el barrio that had never left his soul.

GABRIEL GARCÍA MÁRQUEZ

> **Writer**
> **1927–2014**
> **Heritage: Colombian**

GABRIEL GARCÍA MÁRQUEZ grew up in Aracataca, a small town in the tropics of Colombia, where his parents had left him to be raised by his grandparents while they went to Barranquilla to open a pharmacy.

 His home was rich with stories that would one day shape his own writing—stories filled with magic, history, community, and family.

Gabriel's grandmother was deeply superstitious, and she would regale him with folktales of ghosts and spirits. And his grandfather, a retired colonel, taught Gabriel all about the history of his town and family. Immersed within this landscape of imagination and learning, it was no wonder that Gabriel felt compelled to eventually write his *own* stories!

Before Gabriel turned ten, his beloved grandfather passed away, and he was sent to live with his long-estranged parents. Once the center of his grandparents' worlds, Gabriel was now one of twelve children and felt lonely being thrust back into a home with a family he hardly knew.

Eventually, Gabriel found solace in school, where his aptitude and love for learning flourished. He received a scholarship to a prestigious Jesuit school.

 The more conservative environment was unsettling at first, but Gabriel soon discovered his talent for writing and developed an interest in politics.

He became an avid reader, able to memorize lengthy works of poetry, and his teachers inspired him to take an even greater interest in the politics of his country.

Gabriel left high school determined to use his voice to effect positive change. At the insistence of his father, he enrolled in college to study law, but he soon dropped out and focused instead on his true passion: writing! Gabriel worked as a journalist by day, earning a meager three pesos for each story, while by night he scribbled out poetry and short stories. During this time, Colombia was entrenched in an era of unrest that would come to be known as La Violencia (The Violence). The hardships Gabriel witnessed only further motivated him to give voice to the suffering he saw all around. In 1955, one of his stories upset the country's dictator, and he was forced into exile. That same year, he published his first novel, *La Hojarasca* (*Leaf Storm*).

In 1961, Gabriel and his family moved to Mexico City.

 After a four-year hiatus from writing fiction, he was inspired to write a new story, one that would change his life forever.

Gabriel spent the next eighteen months working feverishly on the novel. Neglecting his work as a journalist, he amassed thousands of dollars in debt and sold his valuable possessions to support his family. When he finally finished the book, Gabriel had to mail his manuscript in two parts because he couldn't afford the postage required to send it to his publisher all at once. But his trials paid off. The book, *Cien Años de Soledad* (*One Hundred Years of Solitude*), was not only published but was such a hit that all the copies sold out in just one week!

Cien Años de Soledad went on to sell millions of copies and was translated into dozens of languages. The book captivated global audiences with its use of magical realism—a blending of reality with supernatural elements, much like the stories Gabriel had loved as a child. He went on to write several other bestselling novels, enchanting his readers with stories that combined serious topics with a touch of fantasy.

In 1982, Gabriel was awarded the Nobel Prize in Literature for creating so many cherished additions to the literary canon. His stories were at once fantastical and profoundly insightful, shining a light on the political dramas that swept through Latin America. He lived as he wrote—speaking out against corruption—and was beloved by his compatriots as an ever-enduring symbol of national pride.

CÉSAR MILSTEIN

{ **Biochemist**
1927–2002
Heritage: Argentinean }

CÉSAR MILSTEIN's fascination with science emerged when he was eight years old. He loved to read and had just finished a book called *Microbe Hunters* when he spoke with a cousin who was developing a treatment for snakebites, igniting César's interest in how people's bodies fight disease.

> It wasn't until many years later that he would learn the full intricacies of the human immune system, but as a child, he was already hooked.

César wanted his future to be in science.

After graduating from high school in Buenos Aires, César enrolled in college to study chemistry. He was brilliant in science, but his grades did not always reflect his abilities. The pull of political activism on campus often made it difficult for him to remain focused on his academic work. César's parents were progressive Jews who raised him with a social conscience. In spite of the disruption to his studies, he often found himself speaking out against a government that supported neither scientific research nor free public education. When he was twenty-four, César was elected student body president during a time when student activists were routinely being arrested.

> Still, he graduated and went on to earn a PhD, which won him an Argentine Chemical Society award for best thesis!

In 1958, César accepted a fellowship from the British Council and moved to Cambridge, England, to pursue the question that had motivated him since childhood: How does the human body fight disease? Within just two years, he earned a second doctoral degree from Cambridge University, and in 1961, he moved back to Argentina to run the new Department of Molecular Biology at the Malbrán Institute. Soon after, the fall of the government—which has been viewed as anti-academic—allowed many other scientists to return home, but it was only a temporary respite. The new government was overthrown and replaced by yet another regime hostile toward academia. As an openly liberal, Jewish academic, César chose to return to Cambridge, where he was allowed to flourish intellectually without constraints on how or what he could study.

Surrounded by renowned scientists such as Francis Crick and Sydney Brenner, César turned his focus to the study of antibodies—the protein molecules in our bodies that defend against foreign entities (like germs). Though scientists had long known that antibodies fought disease, they did not yet understand *how*. César was determined to find out.

Over the next several years, César became internationally recognized for his antibody research. He began working with a former postdoctoral fellow named Georges Köhler. Together, they developed a revolutionary technique that gave scientists the ability to both diagnose and destroy disease-causing antigens using special proteins called *monoclonal antibodies*.

> The scientific community was impressed: César and Georges had unlocked one of the long-held mysteries of the human immune system!

Their pioneering work was published in 1975 in the scientific journal *Nature* and went on to win them and their colleague, Niels Jerne, the 1984 Nobel Prize in Physiology or Medicine. But César's work had just begun—there was still much to learn about the *implications* of this breakthrough.

During the following decades, monoclonal antibodies quickly began to revolutionize the study of medicine. They could be used to test for diseases and blood types, to determine pregnancy, to detect biological weaponry, and even to search for life on other planets. But perhaps most profoundly, César's research allowed for the development of disease-fighting treatments, helping reduce the number of human deaths caused by harmful bacteria and viruses, such as Ebola.

Thanks to César's early fascination with immunology, the world gained powerful knowledge of how human antibodies fight disease. His discoveries led to revolutionary, lifesaving treatments and diagnostic tools. His constant pursuit of academic research, despite an ever-changing political landscape, helped fuel a tide of intellectual discovery that would, ultimately, change the world.

DOLORES HUERTA

Labor Organizer and Activist
1930–
Heritage: Mexican

"Sí se puede"—"yes, it can be done"—was the theme of **DOLORES HUERTA**'s childhood. Her parents were hard workers who never let circumstances hinder their can-do attitude. Dolores's father was a miner and farmworker turned activist and state legislator. Her mother—a single parent of three—always modeled compassion, offering rooms at the hotel she owned in Stockton, California, to low-wage laborers for free and working with her church and community organizations to promote equality and diversity.

It was this commitment to helping others, no matter the obstacles, that Dolores inherited from her parents.

Inspired by their activism, Dolores joined numerous clubs (including the Girl Scouts) at school. She worked hard to earn good grades, believing in herself and her potential even when others didn't. Once, a teacher accused Dolores of cheating because her essays were "too well written" for a Latina. Although frustrated, her determination to succeed in the face of blatant prejudice only made Dolores work harder. "Sí se puede" was the rhythm of her childhood—and her soul.

After graduating from high school, Dolores became an elementary school teacher in Stockton, where she was raised. But she was shaken by the poverty and hunger she witnessed so many of her students struggling with. Their parents, who were farmworkers, were living and working in deplorable conditions, toiling in the fields without breaks, proper toilets, or decent water—all for just seventy cents an hour! Dolores decided that something had to be done. She left teaching to join the Stockton Community Service Organization, where she helped in their push for fair labor and living conditions for farmworkers.

It was there that Dolores met fellow activist Cesar Chavez, and the two became a powerful team.

Together, they formed the National Farm Workers Association (NFWA) and began fighting for farmworkers' rights.

In 1963, Dolores and the NFWA won their first landmark battle when Dolores, a fierce negotiator, secured disability insurance and Aid for Dependent Families—a grant program previously extended only to single parents—for farmworkers in California.

Just two years later, Dolores organized a strike of five thousand grape workers and a nationwide boycott that eventually led to the first contract between the California table grape industry and its workers.

The following decade, she orchestrated another boycott that resulted in groundbreaking legislation: For the first time, farmworkers were allowed to form unions so they could bargain for better working conditions and wages!

But perhaps one of the most iconic moments of Dolores's career came while organizing against an Arizona law that imprisoned people for peaceful protest. While speaking to a group of professionals, Dolores found herself constantly confronted by people saying "no se puede"—"you can't do that!" Just as her parents had done, Dolores rallied against such negativity.

"Sí se puede!" she insisted. "Yes, it can be done!"

This phrase would later become a powerful rallying cry for immigrant rights.

Dolores's many successes were not won easily. Throughout her many years of outspoken activism, she faced both sexism and violence. At the age of fifty-eight, she suffered life-threatening injuries from a police assault on the picket line. After a lengthy recovery, and still refusing to give up, she turned her focus to organizing the next generation of leaders. Dolores spent two years traveling the country, encouraging Latinas to run for office—advocacy that resulted in a significant increase of women representatives in government. She also worked to help elect high-profile allies such as Robert F. Kennedy, Bill Clinton, and Hillary Clinton. She went on to found the Dolores Huerta Foundation, which, among other things, advocates for new leadership in low-income communities.

In 2012, Dolores received the prestigious Presidential Medal of Freedom for her ongoing championing of human rights. Through her tireless activism, Dolores has amplified the voices of previously underrepresented, working-class communities by helping pass new legislation, organize unions, and elect new leaders. Among her many accomplishments, one beat has rung loud in Dolores's life: "sí se puede!"—a rally to justice that echoes on in countless peaceful protests even today.

JAIME ESCALANTE

PUBLIC SCHOOL TEACHER
1930–2010
HERITAGE: BOLIVIAN

To **JAIME ESCALANTE**, a good teacher had the power to transform people's lives for the better. Jaime grew up in poverty in the villages of Bolivia, where both of his parents were public school teachers. He studied to become a teacher, as well, but when he moved to the United States, his credentials were not valid. Jaime found work as a dishwasher and a cook, but he missed doing what he really loved. Determined to find his way back to the classroom, he went back to school to become certified to teach in the United States.

After earning his credentials, Jaime got a job as a teacher at Garfield High School, a predominantly Latine public school in East Los Angeles. The school was performing so far below educational standards that it was in danger of losing its accreditation. And the students, unused to being taken seriously in the classroom—or outside it—were often unruly and disrespectful. Many came from families forced to contend with poverty, violence, and societal neglect. They couldn't see why their education mattered at all in a world that devalued their very existence.

Jaime couldn't fix systemic racism or poverty, but he knew that he *could* help his students find meaning in their studies. He wanted them to believe in themselves as much as he believed in them.

> Jaime was adamant that all his students needed to succeed was ganas—a real *desire* to work hard and rise to the challenges he was prepared to give them.

He pushed the administration to move beyond remedial learning and offer tougher classes. He began teaching algebra and advanced placement (AP) calculus and worked hard to inspire ganas in his students. He wore funny hats, used props, made jokes—anything to get their attention. Jaime's methods, though sometimes unorthodox, had amazing results. His students were finally interested in the course material!

Jaime's first calculus class was tiny—only five students. But they each studied hard for the AP exam, and four of them passed with flying colors, earning college credits for their scores. Jaime was so inspired by this success that he worked to recruit more students, offering after-school sessions and Saturday classes to prepare them for the difficult exam. He tutored those who needed extra help, working with them before school and during his lunch hour.

> At the end of the year, Jaime's class of eighteen took the AP test at last—and every student passed!

Jaime was proud of his students, but others were skeptical. The Educational Testing Service, which oversaw the exam, accused Jaime's class of cheating. They could not believe that the impoverished Latine students of Garfield High could possibly have passed such a difficult test on their own merits. Jaime was furious, but he would not accept such blatant discrimination. He convinced his students to take the exam again, and, again, every one of them passed. The students of Garfield finally had an advocate to show them—and the world—their incredible potential!

> The story of Jaime and his students garnered national attention, leading to corporate and nonprofit funding that changed the future of Garfield High School forever.

The school now had money to hire tutors, purchase computers and audiovisual equipment, and offer college scholarships to its graduates. Within a decade, students were able to take AP classes in fourteen different subjects—calculus among them. The ganas of Jaime and his students had transformed an entire community. Together, they proved that every student, no matter their ethnicity or income level, could flourish with the help of someone who truly believed in them.

RITA MORENO

{ Actor, Singer, and Dancer
1931–
Heritage: Puerto Rican }

RITA MORENO loved to perform even when she was little. She lived on a farm with her family near the El Yunque rainforest in Puerto Rico. And though Rita was far away from the buzz of city life, she felt called to the stage and would often put on dance shows for her grandfather in their home. But everything changed when Rita was five, and her parents decided to divorce. She moved to New York with her mother, leaving her brother behind and embarking on a strange new life.

Though Rita felt lonely in the unfamiliar city, she found comfort in performing. She began taking dance classes after one of her mother's friends took notice of her talent. It wasn't long before Rita was auditioning for parts for radio and film, and she was dubbing Spanish-language versions of American movies by the age of eleven. When she was thirteen, Rita made her Broadway debut in a production called *Skydrift*. Soon, she was receiving offers from Hollywood agents, all of whom saw that Rita had a bright future in entertainment. In 1950, she landed her first movie role in a film called *So Young, So Bad*. But her big break came when she signed a seven-year contract with the world-famous MGM Studios.

Rita moved to California to pursue her dream of becoming a successful actress.

> She was offered small parts in several films, but she was disappointed to find that Hollywood was entrenched in stereotypes, and she was often relegated to typecast roles.

Even though she was Puerto Rican, Hollywood treated her like a kind of cultural chameleon. She was cast as characters who were Hawaiian, Egyptian, Indigenous American, Filipina, and Burmese—despite the fact that she knew next to nothing about any of these cultures or how best to portray them! Rita felt demeaned by the film industry's inability to see past her cultural heritage and by the assumption that all non-white people were the same. Nonetheless, she persisted in the belief that her talent would *someday* be recognized.

In 1961, Rita's perseverance finally paid off when she was cast as Anita in *West Side Story*, a movie about Puerto Rican transplants to New York.

> For her work in the film, Rita earned an Academy Award for Best Supporting Actress, which enabled her to, at last, be seen for the passionate and talented Latina actress she was.

She was elated, convinced that the doors once closed to her would now be opened, but she was soon disappointed to discover that her casting prospects had not improved whatsoever.

Frustrated by Hollywood's continued insistence on offering her stereotyped roles, Rita turned her focus to theater, returning to her roots on Broadway. She began dividing her time between the stage and television, starring in the children's show *The Electric Company*, for which she won a Grammy. In 1975, Rita added a Tony Award (for her stunning performance in the Broadway production of *The Ritz*) to her growing list of accolades. Two years later, she accepted an Emmy Award for her appearance on *The Muppet Show*, becoming the first Latina to receive all four major entertainment awards and receive EGOT status!

Despite the outdated thinking of a film industry steeped in bias, Rita never lost her innate passion for performing. Her stunning career as a triple threat—actress, dancer, and singer—has spanned more than seven decades, paving the way for future Latine performers. Her contributions to the arts have earned her countless Lifetime Achievement awards, as well as the Presidential Medal of Freedom and the National Medal of Arts. The wisdom she imparted to those who would follow in her footsteps is crystal clear: No matter what obstacles stand in your way, don't give up. Keep believing in yourself! Rita showed the world what it meant to persevere in the face of systemic prejudice, pushing back against those who kept her down to achieve what she always believed she could.

WALTER MERCADO

Astrologer and TV Personality
1932–2019
Heritage: Puerto Rican

WALTER MERCADO always felt different, but his mother taught him from a young age that being unique is a gift, not something to be ashamed of. Growing up, his brother spent time out in the fields with his father, riding horses and planting sugarcane, but Walter preferred to stay home, playing piano and reading books. He was once moved by the plight of an injured bird that had flown into his yard. Gently, Walter picked up the bird and began to caress it—and, magically, the bird took flight!

A neighbor who had been watching spread word of the miracle: Walter had healing powers!

Soon, people began lining up at his door to be touched by his gift. Yes, Walter was different, but in ways that gave people hope for a better life.

Embracing his artistic inclinations, Walter trained as a dancer and began acting in theater productions and, eventually, telenovelas (Spanish-language soap operas). One day, he was asked to appear on a talk show to promote a play he was in, but when one of the show's other guests dropped out, Walter stepped in to take his place.

He had come dressed in a long white robe and dazzling makeup, and he spent the entire show talking passionately about astrology instead of his play.

No one had ever seen anything like it. Who was this mystical man? The station was flooded with calls from viewers who wanted more Walter Mercado!

Walter was asked to star in a daily fifteen-minute TV segment, where he appeared wearing extravagant capes with flashy jewelry, big hair, and shimmering makeup—defying traditional gender norms with unapologetic bravado. He waved his hands in graceful motions as he told peoples' horoscopes, enchanting the viewers at home with his endless positivity and messages of unconditional love.

It was not long before Walter's influence extended beyond Puerto Rico. He was soon captivating audiences across Latin America, the United States, and Europe.

His fifteen-minute segment became a popular one-hour show—the first show in history dedicated solely to astrology. He began making radio appearances in addition and soon became the most recognizable celebrity psychic in the world. At the peak of his career, Walter had over 120 million viewers! But an unexpected betrayal would change Walter's life and career forever.

In 2006, Walter's show was taken off the air after more than fifteen years, when he inadvertently signed a contract that turned over his name and brand to his manager. The betrayal was costly—not only financially but emotionally and physically, as well. Though Walter eventually won the lawsuit, he had lost six precious years of his career and suffered a stress-induced heart attack. He remained off the air until, in 2020, a documentary called *Mucho Mucho Amor* was released, detailing Walter's life and revitalizing his legacy. The title of the film was based on the daily message Walter imparted to his audience, encouraging them to live their lives with "lots and lots of love."

His unshakable positivity was coupled with a consistent challenge to notions of gender, which gave hope to many viewers who also sought freedom from traditional gender norms.

With his staunch refusal to conform, Walter's ultimate legacy was one of acceptance. He taught others to embrace their differences with mucho mucho amor.

ROBERTO CLEMENTE

{ Baseball Player
1934–1972
Heritage: Puerto Rican }

The youngest of seven children born to working-class parents in Puerto Rico, **ROBERTO CLEMENTE** was proud of who he was and where he came from. He knew what it was to work hard and still struggle to put food on the table. His father was a foreman in the sugarcane fields, and his mother worked tirelessly as a laundress. But despite their hardships, they believed in staying humble and caring for the needs of others. From a young age, Roberto often helped his family by doing odd jobs and working in the fields with his father.

In his free time, Roberto enjoyed playing sports and even made his own baseballs by filling socks with pebbles.

In high school, he excelled in the high jump and javelin and was considered a contender for the Olympics. But Roberto's true passion was always baseball. He idolized Monte Irvin, a famous left fielder who played with the San Juan Senators, and would often carry the player's bags to get free entry to games, dreaming all the while of the day he would get the chance to play.

By the time Roberto was seventeen, he was playing with the Puerto Rican Baseball League. Just a year later, he was scouted to play in the minor leagues with the Brooklyn Dodgers. Roberto was given a $10,000 bonus, which was a lot of money at the time—but his talents were wasted with the Dodgers, who rarely let him play. The following year, however, he was traded to the Pittsburgh Pirates.

At last, Roberto would be playing in the majors, his talent on display for the whole world to see!

Roberto was a powerful right fielder, with a fierce throwing arm and an impressive batting average. But he faced an uphill battle—with injuries, as well as discrimination. Roberto was mocked by the press for his heavy Puerto Rican accent, and he was often confronted with the ugly reality of racial segregation. At spring training, he and other Black players had to stay on the bus while their teammates ate at "whites-only" restaurants. Roberto found this unacceptable and demanded that the Pirates provide separate transportation for the Black players so they could find restaurants where they were welcome.

Though he was unfairly forced to navigate daily injustices, Roberto's talent was undeniable, and he quickly became a star on the field.

Over the next several years, he won four National League batting titles and twelve consecutive Golden Glove Awards.

In 1966, he was awarded the league title of Most Valuable Player. He led the Pirates to the World Series twice—first in 1960 and again in 1971—and in 1972, he became the eleventh player in baseball history to achieve the milestone of three thousand career hits.

With his unstoppable arm and unmatched speed, Roberto was a force to be reckoned with—on and off the field. An unapologetic advocate for social justice, he took every opportunity to fight for equal treatment of Latine players and spent the off-season at home in Puerto Rico giving baseball clinics to underprivileged children.

Roberto dreamed of a world where all people, regardless of their race or nationality, would be given the same opportunities to succeed in life, and he did everything he could to help make that dream a reality.

In 1972, following a devastating earthquake in Nicaragua, Roberto boarded a plane to assist with relief efforts. Tragically, the plane crashed, and Roberto was killed at the young age of thirty-eight, leaving behind an unforgettable legacy of generosity and sportsmanship. The year after his death, he became the first Latine player to be inducted into the Baseball Hall of Fame, his achievement flying in the face of the rule requiring five years between a player's death and their induction. In honor of both his outstanding athleticism and his humanitarian spirit, every year the Major League Baseball Players Association awards a player the Roberto Clemente Award for exemplary sportsmanship and community service. Roberto gave his all to the sport of baseball while also carrying with him an enduring compassion for others and an unwavering dream of a better world.

SYLVIA MENDEZ

Activist
1936–
Heritage: Mexican

SYLVIA MENDEZ grew up during a time when racial segregation was the norm in the United States. When she was eight years old, her family moved to Westminster County in California, where they leased a farm from a Japanese family that had been incarcerated in a camp during World War II.

> When Sylvia and her siblings tried to enroll in the school their father had attended, they were turned away—but their lighter-skinned cousins were allowed to register.

Her aunt, incensed by this blatant display of institutional racism, refused to accept it. She left with *all* the kids and marched home to share the news with Sylvia's parents. The Seventeenth Street School, with its groomed lawns and beautiful open-air playground, would not enroll children with dark skin—it was for white students only.

Sylvia and her sisters had no choice but to attend the underfunded "Mexican school" down the street, which consisted of two wooden shacks and offered little to its students in the way of education. Enclosed by an electric fence, the school was adjacent to a cow pasture; all the books were secondhand, and the desks were in a state of disrepair. Instead of learning how to read and write, the students were prepared for work—boys were trained for physical labor, and girls were taught to be domestic workers.

> Sylvia spent her days dreaming of the properly funded school that the white kids were allowed to attend. But her parents were not satisfied with wishful thinking. Instead, they prepared to *fight*.

While Sylvia's mother took over the farm, her father hired a civil rights lawyer and, at the lawyer's suggestion, recruited four other families to file a class action lawsuit against the Orange County school districts they each came from. The case, *Mendez v. Westminster*, represented thousands of Mexican American children who, just like Sylvia and her siblings, had been victims of unconstitutional discrimination.

Though Sylvia attended court each day, she was too young to really understand the proceedings. All she knew was that she wished she could go to a school where she could learn and play. In 1946, in a landmark ruling, the court ruled in favor of Sylvia's family.

> Public schools in Orange County—and in *all* of California—were forced to desegregate!

Sylvia was finally allowed to enroll in the Seventeenth Street School, but her hard-won elation was soon overshadowed by the daily bullying she faced: Her peers singled her out and ridiculed her for being Mexican and having dark skin. Eventually, Sylvia told her mother that she wanted to leave school altogether. In response, her mother was kind but firm. She reminded Sylvia that the fight they had won had been not just for her but for *all* brown-skinned children.

Sylvia continued going to school in spite of the daily challenges. A decade later, a new case was filed in a different part of the country.

> *Brown v. Board of Education* brought an end to school segregation across the entire United States—a tremendous achievement made possible by the precedent set by Sylvia's case.

Though Sylvia's family went largely overlooked for many years, their story re-emerged after Sylvia—at the insistence of her dying mother—began speaking about it publicly. A retired nurse of thirty-three years, she traveled all over the country talking to students about the landmark case that had changed the course of US history. Films and books documented the story of Sylvia and her family—and, in 2011, Sylvia was awarded the Presidential Medal of Freedom. As President Barack Obama presented her with the award, she could not help but cry. Her family—champions in the fight for equality—had at last been acknowledged for their role in desegregating schools and championing equal education for all children.

FLORENTINA LÓPEZ DE JESÚS

{ Artisan and Activist
1939–2014
Heritage: Mexican }

Like the many generations of Indigenous Amuzgo women from the Mexican state of Guerrero who had come before her, **FLORENTINA LÓPEZ DE JESÚS** was an expert artisan. When Florentina was six, her mother taught her to pick, spin, and weave cotton, skills passed from mother to daughter in her family for generations.

Weaving was a way of life for many Amuzgo women, both as a part of their cultural history and as a way to produce income.

For Florentina, weaving would also become a way to preserve her community's traditions long into the future.

When Florentina was fourteen, she ventured to the city of Ometepec to take a job as a domestic worker, hoping to help her parents support their family of seven. While working in Ometepec, she learned to read and write in both Spanish and Amuzgo. She also began using her creative talents to make goods to sell at the market. Florentina made beautiful napkins, tablecloths, and shawls and finely crafted huipiles (traditional Indigenous cotton dresses woven on a backstrap loom).

Her gorgeous creations quickly caught the attention of FONART, a government agency that represented Mexican artists and that eventually helped her sell her art for a fair price.

But Florentina was not the only one who needed help selling her wares. The weavers in her community were being paid very little due to low market rates in neighboring Acapulco. Florentina became concerned that the quality of her community's textiles would suffer as the weavers struggled to produce more work faster just to make ends meet. To remedy the issue, she assembled a group of eleven Amuzgo weavers and formed the Flor de Xochistlahuaca cooperative. Together, they focused their efforts on promoting Amuzgo art and identity, leading workshops and seminars to teach younger generations the skills of traditional dyeing and weaving.

In the 1970s, Florentina's cooperative received the support of Luis Echeverría, the president of Mexico, who helped showcase and preserve traditional Mexican art. He decorated his home with Mexican crafts, gave folk art to foreign dignitaries, and had members of his cabinet dress in Native regalia for important state receptions. He also commissioned the Xochistlahuaca cooperative to weave six hundred tablecloths and napkins—an effort that Florentina organized, overseeing quality control and production.

By 2001, Florentina's cooperative had grown to include dozens of weavers, and Florentina herself had become known as an expert weaver! She won numerous awards and prizes, including the United Nations Educational, Scientific and Cultural Organization (UNESCO) Crafts Prize and the FONART Popular Art Grand Prize, and participated in the Great Masters of Mexican Popular Art exhibition, where her work captivated the Spanish monarch Queen Sofia.

Florentina used her global platform to advocate publicly for the rights of Indigenous women.

She was twice elected as a councilwoman in her hometown of Suljaa, where she was well-known for her community activism.

Throughout her lifetime, Florentina gave voice to the disenfranchised members of her community, working hard to preserve their traditions and advocating for just treatment, especially of Indigenous women.

Though she had no children of her own, she was like a mother to many within her community, passing along the artisanal skills her mother had taught her as a child.

Because of Florentina's efforts, the weaving traditions of the Amuzgo continue to thrive, and the generations that have followed have the tools to carry on in her footsteps.

MARIA BUENO

Tennis Player
1939–2018
Heritage: Brazilian

Born to a family of tennis enthusiasts, **MARIA BUENO** first picked up a tennis racket when she was only six years old. Her parents loved the sport, and the whole family would play together regularly on the clay courts across the street from their home in São Paulo.

Even though Maria had an innate gift, playing with power and grace, she was given no formal training and learned to play on instinct. She loved swooping to the net and delivering killer shots!

Maria won her first tennis tournament at the age of twelve, and she began competing internationally two years later.

When she was only fifteen years old, Maria won the women's tennis championship of Brazil, becoming so formidable on the court that grown men were afraid to play against her!

Winning the championship gave Maria a taste of just how good she could be, but she soon became hungry for new challenges and traveled to competitions outside Brazil. During her first year of touring, she worked so hard, she lost more than seventeen pounds. Being away from her family was hard, but Maria was determined—she loved the game!

As word of Maria's remarkable skill spread, she began playing exhibition matches. She beat greats such as Darlene Hard and Althea Gibson, some of the best tennis players in the United States.

With these wins, Maria started to think she might actually have what it took to become the best tennis player in the world!

In 1959, she won the singles title at both Wimbledon *and* the US Nationals. She would ultimately win a stunning total of nineteen Grand Slam titles. Maria's dream soon came true. She was ranked the number one tennis player in the world—a title she proudly held on to for much of the 1960s!

Maria's playing caught the eye of the press, who likened her to a ballerina on the court. She attracted admiring new fans to the sport of women's tennis with her unmatched athleticism, and her unique fashion sense also set Maria apart from other players of the time.

She brought style to the game, donning athletic tennis dresses specially designed for her.

Her attire was chic and glamorous—and sometimes scandalously edgy. Maria drew gasps from the conservative Wimbledon crowd when she wore a white skirt lined with pink, leading the club to enforce a strict "white skirts only" dress code. She was stylish, graceful, and powerful on the court—a winning combination that earned her nicknames like the Latin Sliver of Fire and Ice and the São Paulo Swallow.

Maria's career was thrilling, but it wasn't always easy. On several occasions, her intense training made her susceptible to illness and injury that left her bedridden for months. In 1967, she destroyed her arm at Wimbledon after playing 120 back-to-back games. She was told by her doctors that she would never play again, but Maria could not imagine her life without tennis. She would not be defeated!

After seven years of surgery and rehabilitation, Maria finally returned to the court.

She made a stunning comeback when she won the Japan Open, a world-renowned tennis tournament, in the mid-'70s.

She returned to Wimbledon in 1976 and 1977, making it all the way to the quarterfinals despite the damage to her arm. Maria spent the latter part of her career giving clinics and commentating, returning to the court from time to time to compete as a senior. She never lost her love of the game, and in 2004, she was inducted into the International Women's Sports Hall of Fame. Maria brought power and flair to a sport formerly dominated by men, her stunning career blazing a trail for women athletes all over the world.

JOAN BAEZ

{ Singer and Activist
1941–
Heritage: Mexican }

JOAN BAEZ found both her voice and her place in the world through music. As a kid, Joan often had trouble navigating a culturally divided playground. Half Mexican and half Scottish, she didn't quite fit in with either the white children *or* the Latine children in her Staten Island neighborhood. The pervasive sense of loneliness that came from feeling like an outsider, coupled with her ongoing anxiety attacks, only made it harder to make friends.

But when she sang in the choir at school or played her ukulele, Joan felt seen at last. She had a *voice*, and she had something to say!

Joan's father was a physicist whose research took him to many different places, from New York to California to Iraq, where Joan witnessed the harsh effects of poverty firsthand. It was during these years that she developed a deep social conscience.

What better way to communicate the struggles of marginalized people, she thought, than through music?

In 1954, when Joan was thirteen, her aunt and uncle took her to see folk singer Pete Seeger in concert. She was enthralled by his roots rock, blue-collar songs, which were so different from the popular music of the time. Joan decided she wanted to become a folk singer, too. She spent the next four years learning to play the guitar and practicing folk songs. After high school, her family moved to Boston, where folk music was taking off. She was enamored by the warm acoustic vibe of the coffee shop scene, where aspiring folk singers gathered to share inspiration. While her father taught at the Massachusetts Institute of Technology (MIT), Joan began studying theater at Boston University, but she hated the experience and, instead, turned her focus to music.

Joan's first gig was at Club 47, where she played barefoot to a small crowd of friends. She was paid a mere ten dollars, but Joan was thrilled just to be doing what she loved. She continued performing at venues throughout the city and quickly grew a loyal following.

In 1959, she caught her first big break when folk icon Bob Gibson invited her onstage at the Newport Folk Festival.

Joan was a hit! The audience loved her beautiful soprano voice. Afterward, she was courted by the major record label Columbia Records, whose offer she turned down in favor of the less commercial Vanguard Records. She released her first album, entitled *Joan Baez*, in 1960 and quickly emerged as a powerful force within the folk revival movement.

Not long after the release of her debut album, Joan met Bob Dylan at a club in Greenwich Village. Captivated by his songs, she became instrumental in helping introduce his talents to wider audiences. Together, they became the social conscience of the music world, performing timely songs with messages of civil rights, social justice, and nonviolence.

In an era of war and social unrest, Joan was determined to use her voice for change. She performed at anti-Vietnam War rallies and participated in the free speech movement at the University of California, Berkeley. In 1963, she sang "We Shall Overcome" at the March on Washington, the event where Martin Luther King Jr. gave his historic "I Have a Dream" speech. During the same decade, Joan cofounded a school for peace in California called the Institute for the Study of Nonviolence and helped the human rights organization Amnesty International establish its West Coast branch.

Joan never stopped recording, performing, and advocating for social justice. Over the course of six decades, she released more than thirty multi-award-winning albums, charting in the United States and abroad with songs like "Diamonds and Rust" and "Where Are You Now, My Son?"

In 2007, Joan was honored by the Recording Academy with a Grammy Lifetime Achievement Award.

Her debut album was inducted into the Grammy Hall of Fame and subsequently preserved by the Library of Congress in the National Recording Registry. In 2015, she was bestowed the Ambassador of Conscience Award by Amnesty International for her lifelong service to the fight for human rights and advancement of peace around the world.

Though Joan had once struggled to find her voice, once she found it, she was unstoppable! She has used it to change both music *and* the world.

Her heartrending songs and immovable conscience have made her an icon for the ages, influencing generations of singers, songwriters, and activists.

She helped lead the world through an era of protest with the power of her voice and words, never giving up on the fight for social justice.

EDSON ARANTES DO NASCIMENTO
(PELÉ)

Footballer/Soccer Player
1940–2022
Heritage: Brazilian

EDSON ARANTES DO NASCIMENTO—or **PELÉ**, as he would later be known—always knew he had a special gift for playing football (known as *soccer* in the United States). He could kick the ball with power and precision in a way other kids couldn't. It was tempting to boast, but his father, who made a living playing football, taught Pelé that this talent was a gift he would someday be able to use to help others.

Growing up in a working-class family in Três Corações, Brazil, Pelé knew firsthand what it was like to struggle. His father made very little money playing football, so Pelé had to work from a young age. He supplemented his family's income by shining shoes and selling meat pies, imagining a day when children like him, all over the world, would be free from the hardships of poverty.

> 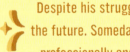 Despite his struggles, Pelé's talent gave him hope for the future. Someday, he dreamed, he would play football professionally and win the World Cup for his country.

When Pelé was fifteen, he won the Junior Victory Cup at his local athletic club and was then recruited to play for the Santos Football Club, which took note of his talent. He helped the Santos team win nine league championships, the Libertadores Cup, and the Intercontinental Club Cup before he was recruited to play with the Brazilian national football team at the 1958 World Cup.

> With Pelé's prodigious talent, Brazil won, and Pelé became a national hero. Because of *him*, Brazil had become known as a serious football country!

Pelé was a ray of hope for a country in political turmoil. Now recognized across the world, he began fielding offers to play football outside Brazil. But Brazil's president was not keen to let him go and named Pelé a national treasure, which legally prohibited him from leaving the country for several years. Instead of seeing this as a setback, in 1962, Pelé helped his team win the World Cup again, despite sustaining an injury that forced him to sit out part of the tournament.

> His ability to score crowd-pleasing goals launched Pelé to international superstardom—and made him one of the most revered athletes in history.

In 1967, Pelé was changed forever after traveling to Nigeria. The civil war-torn country called a temporary ceasefire just to watch Pelé play! This experience reaffirmed what he had already long known—that sports could bring about positive change. He resolved to use his platform to help those in need however he could. Just two years later, when Pelé scored his one-thousandth goal, he tearfully dedicated it to the street children of Brazil. In 1972, he renegotiated his contract and agreed to donate his entire salary to charity for one year. When Pelé finally left Brazil to play football for the Cosmos in the United States, he made sure that his new contract enabled him to found a soccer school for impoverished Brazilian children.

> For all his charitable efforts, in 1994, Pelé was appointed Champion for Sport by the United Nations Educational, Scientific and Cultural Organization (UNESCO).

Pelé's unmatched athleticism earned him countless honors, from being named Footballer of the Century to receiving an honorary knighthood from Queen Elizabeth II of England. His unrivaled power on the field drew new fans to the sport from all around the world. And although he became one of the most beloved athletes of all time, Pelé never forgot the early lessons of his childhood. His talent was a gift—one he used not just in service of his own dreams but also to help level the playing field for children everywhere.

MARIO J. MOLINA

{ **Chemist**
1943–2020
Heritage: Mexican }

Even as a child, **MARIO J. MOLINA** was fascinated by science. He was given a toy microscope, which he loved using to examine single-celled organisms. As his curiosity grew, Mario turned his family's bathroom into a makeshift laboratory and spent hours conducting his own experiments. His aunt Esther, who was a chemist, noticed his fascination with science and helped him conduct more and more challenging experiments. Soon, they were performing experiments at the college level!

Since Mario expressed such an interest in chemistry, his parents made a bold decision.

> **They sent Mario to a boarding school in Switzerland at the age of eleven to help him learn German, the up-and-coming language of the scientific community.**

He went on to study chemical engineering in college, then spent two years researching at the University of Freiburg in Germany before accepting a position as an assistant professor of chemical engineering back in Mexico. But Mario soon found that his scientific curiosity wasn't satisfied. He wanted to continue his own studies, so he enrolled as a PhD student at the University of California, Berkeley, at the height of the civil rights movement.

Mario's time in Berkeley was rich with intellectual and political discourse.

> **He began to think deeply about the impact he could have on society.**

His research included work with chemical lasers, which, in many places, were being developed as weapons. But Mario did not want to cause harm. He wanted to *help* society! In 1973, he began working with Professor F. Sherwood Rowland as a doctoral fellow, researching how industrial chemicals called *chlorofluorocarbons* (CFCs) affected the environment. With Sherwood, he developed the CFC-ozone depletion theory, outlining how CFCs were depleting Earth's ozone layer. The ozone layer is the part of Earth's atmosphere that protects all living beings from solar radiation. Without it, life on Earth would be impossible. Mario and Sherwood knew they had to do something to help.

Together, they published their findings in the scientific journal *Nature*. They reached out to the media and published other papers, doing everything they could to relay the importance of their discovery to policymakers. Their research sparked discourse throughout the United States, but it wasn't until the '80s that the ozone hole Mario and Sherwood predicted was finally discovered above Antarctica. This area of ozone depletion confirmed what they had known for years, and its discovery led to global policy changes that would help protect the environment.

> **Mario's dream of using science to make a positive difference in the world was finally coming true!**

Because of his work, Mario was invited to serve as a science and technology adviser to US presidents Bill Clinton and Barack Obama. In 1995, he, Sherwood, and their colleague Paul J. Crutzen were jointly awarded the Nobel Prize in Chemistry for their contributions to atmospheric chemistry. And in 2013, Mario received the Presidential Medal of Honor for his work combatting climate change.

> **He worked tirelessly until the end of his life to reduce harmful emissions, a true champion of the environment and a hero to all of humanity.**

SUSANA BACA

{ **Singer and Songwriter**
1944–
Heritage: Peruvian }

When she was little, **SUSANA BACA** dreamed of becoming a singer. Susana was raised in a barrio that traced its roots back to slavery during the Spanish Empire. Like the rest of Peru, it was deeply entrenched in a climate of racial inequality. Her family was poor, and her neighborhood lacked electricity, but her childhood was rich with the Afro-Peruvian rhythms of her community—the percussive festejo and the melodic landó that originated from her ancestors in Africa.

> Susana's love of music grew organically from the pulse of her community's social gatherings, where her father played guitar and her mother taught her how to dance.

When friends and neighbors got together, they would play instruments they had made themselves. Susana loved to join in and sing! She wanted to sing for a living, too, but her parents encouraged her to become a teacher instead. Black singers were not welcome in mainstream Peruvian music—yet.

Susana had never thought of herself as being different from anyone else. But then, in high school, she was deliberately left off the dance team due to the dark color of her skin. In that painful moment, Susana decided, once and for all, that something had to be done about the racial prejudice in her country.

> She was *proud* to be Black—to be Afro-Peruvian— and she would show the world why.

Though Susana followed her parents' advice and became a primary school teacher, her heart was pulled back to her deep love of music, and she quit teaching after only three years. She began to study the African roots of her community's music. Susana sought grants that enabled her to perform in small venues throughout Lima and neighboring cities. She traveled across Peru to small towns with large Black populations, learning traditional folk music that she then reinterpreted in her own unique style. Her songs were accompanied by Afro-Peruvian instruments like the cajón, a polished wooden box upon which players sit as they beat out percussive rhythms.

> Her soulful voice and plaintive melodies soon caught the attention of a composer named Chabuca Granda, who helped Susana broker a record deal.

But in 1983, upon Chabuca's sudden death, the deal fell apart.

It wasn't until 1995, when Susana was fifty-one years old, that she finally got her big break: Her version of the song "Maria Landó" was featured on the compilation record *The Soul of Black Peru*! The song, a lyrical account of the suffering of a Black working woman, catapulted Susana to international prominence—taking her message with it. Black music could no longer sit on the sidelines of Peruvian culture. It was as rich and complex and beautiful as it had always been—and now, at last, the rest of the world was appreciating it, too. Susana released a self-titled debut album, followed swiftly by several more, and performed throughout Europe and North America to enchanted audiences. Her songs were full of poetry, blurring the boundaries of genre and infusing the music of her ancestors with contemporary harmonies and rhythms.

In 2002, Susana won a Latin Grammy for Best Folk Album. Nine years later, she won her second Grammy for the song "Latinoamérica," a collaboration with artists Calle 13, Totó la Momposina, and Maria Rita. Bolstered by her success, Susana and her husband founded the Black Continuum Institute—an organization dedicated to the collection, preservation, and creation of Black music and dance. In 2011, she was named Peru's Minister of Culture, making history as the first Black female cabinet member in Peru—and positioning her to help dismantle systems of oppression that harmed her and so many others.

> Susana, the girl from the barrios of Lima, did what no one thought possible.

She became a singer after all, using her talents to work for a better future and sharing the beauty of Afro-Peruvian music with the world!

REVEREND GÉRARD JEAN-JUSTE

Human Rights Activist
1946–2009
Heritage: Haitian

REVEREND GÉRARD JEAN-JUSTE was a man of unwavering conscience who devoted his life to defending the rights of *all* people to live with dignity. Gérard knew from the time he was young that he wanted to become a priest, but the seminaries of Haiti had all been closed by the government, which ruled over the working classes through corruption and military abuses. So, in the late 1960s, Gérard moved to Canada to study, then relocated to the United States, where he became the country's first ordained Haitian priest.

Gérard served as a deacon in Brooklyn, but he soon felt the call to return to his home, where he knew people were suffering beneath the weight of political and economic oppression.

He strongly believed that his mission as a priest was to help the poor and politically subjugated, and he soon became known for refusing to stay silent in the face of injustice.

Gérard was openly critical of the Haitian government, which had a history of maintaining rule through violence, and was forced to return to the United States when he would not swear loyalty to the regime.

While living in the United States, Gérard moved to Miami to advocate for Haitian refugees. He felt the US government was discriminating against them for both racial and political reasons. Not only had the government stood in support of the Haitian dictatorship, but it was refusing to grant asylum to refugees whose lives were at risk if deported back to Haiti.

Although the Haitian and US governments were powerful adversaries to make, Gérard would not be silenced.

He challenged the deportations of Haitian people in the US courts and staged countless public demonstrations. Gérard was fearless in his fight against injustice—even when he could be arrested for it. On one occasion, he even lay down in the street to stop buses from transporting refugees facing deportation!

It wasn't until the Haitian dictatorship fell that, in 1991, Gérard was finally able to move back home. He was excited to lend his support to the first democratically elected president of Haiti: Jean-Bertrand Aristide, a former Catholic priest who shared Gérard's belief in dignity for all people. Sadly, however, Aristide was ousted in a coup just seven months into his presidency, forcing Gérard back into hiding.

The years that followed were hard, but Gérard continued his fight for justice.

He returned to Port au Prince to operate a free soup kitchen, providing much-needed help for many poverty-stricken Haitians. When the Aristide administration fell for the second time, Gérard fought openly against the new government. He became the target of threats of violence and was wrongfully jailed twice, being named a "prisoner of conscience" by Amnesty International.

After six months in prison, Gérard was released to seek treatment for leukemia. But it was too late; the damage to his health had been done. Gérard died three years later in a hospital in Miami. Before his death, he famously told a Haitian court that his rosary (the string of beads he used to count his prayers) was his only weapon.

For the rest of his life, he would fight with conviction for the freedom of the people of Haiti.

To his last breath, Gérard lived his life according to his fierce principles, refusing to give up on the idea that all people could someday be free and happy.

PAULO COELHO

Lyricist and Novelist
1947–
Heritage: Brazilian

PAULO COELHO's family never tolerated the idea that he might grow up to be a writer. Everything in his life was strictly regimented; his parents were both strict Catholics who expected him to study engineering like his father, and they were less than thrilled when he told them he wanted to be an author. They tried everything to dissuade him—first bribing him, then cutting off his allowance. When Paulo could not be swayed, they sent him to a psychiatrist.

But nothing would change his mind. Even at an early age, he had the soul of an artist.

In their unyielding determination to break Paulo of his dream, his parents finally had him committed to a mental institution. He escaped three times, unwilling to let his spirit be pathologized or confined. Upon his release from the institution three long years later, Paulo briefly succumbed to his parents' wishes to return to his education and began to study law. But he would not conform for long. His spirit would not be broken.

Paulo left his law studies after only one year and traveled the world, becoming a self-proclaimed hippie and enjoying the "free" culture of the '60s. He traveled through South America, North Africa, Europe, and the United States, eventually returning home to Brazil to write lyrics for a rock star named Raul Seixas. Paulo began writing songs for musicians who were critical of Brazil's authoritarian government. In 1974, he was thrown in jail for the subversive lyrics he penned. Though Paulo was tortured during his imprisonment, he still would not be broken. He continued his activism, making a living by writing songs for record companies. But Paulo knew something still wasn't right. *Something* was missing in his life. At the age of thirty-nine, he set out to Spain, where he walked a five hundred-mile pilgrimage down the Camino de Santiago. While on the road to the tomb of Saint James, he experienced a spiritual revelation. Paulo realized that, despite his struggles and his successes, he still wasn't fulfilling the dream he'd held since he was a child.

It was finally time to listen to his heart. It was time to write.

In 1986, Paulo quit his other jobs to begin writing fiction in earnest. He published *The Pilgrimage* (originally titled *O Diário de um Mago* [*Diary of a Magus*]) in 1987, but it met with little success. Facing doubt about his future as a full-time author, Paulo asked for a sign from God: If he saw a white feather, he would write a new book. He received his sign that very day—a white feather in the window of a store—and recommitted himself to writing. The following year, Paulo finished his most promising work, a novel called *O Alquimista* (*The Alchemist*). The book, which chronicled a shepherd boy's journey across North Africa in search of treasure, was published in 1988 by a small Brazilian press that printed only nine hundred copies and decided against a second printing. But with the warmer reception of his following novel, *Brida*, Paulo was given another chance.

A large publisher in the United States took an interest in *The Alchemist* and reissued the book.

This time, it became an international sensation, selling thirty-five million copies in countries all around the world! Paulo was thrilled. At last, he could afford to become a full-time writer and devote himself to what he loved most.

Paulo continued writing, publishing new work nearly every two years. His books have been published in more than 170 countries, garnering international acclaim. He even received the Guinness World Record for most translations of a single title signed in one sitting by a living author! Paulo had wanted his work to make a difference in the world long before achieving his dream, and he could now use his international platform to fight for marginalized voices. In 1996, he founded the Paulo Coelho Institute to provide support to children and the elderly.

And in 2007, the United Nations named Paulo a Messenger of Peace, honoring his unique ability to inspire people around the globe profoundly with his words.

In spite of the challenges of his early years, Paulo never gave up on himself or his dream. He *knew* who he was, and he persevered with undaunted tenacity—a gift to the millions of readers who find solace in his books and in the power of his voice.

FRANKLIN CHANG-DÍAZ

Astronaut and Physicist
1950–
Heritage: Costa Rican

FRANKLIN CHANG-DÍAZ grew up during the earliest years of space exploration, dreaming that one day, he, too, might see the stars from the window of a spaceship. He loved to pretend that his cardboard box was a real-life rocket, counting down: *Three . . . two . . . one . . . blastoff!* And off he would go on his first space mission!

Franklin knew that the journey to space would come with many challenges. His parents had little in the way of money, and neither had gone to college. Plus, there had never been any astronauts who looked like Franklin, who was Chinese on his father's side and Costa Rican on his mother's side. But he was determined.

After graduating from high school, he left Costa Rica and moved to the United States, the only place where Franklin knew he could get the training he needed to become an astronaut.

He reenrolled in high school, starting all over again so he could apply to college in the United States. But Franklin didn't speak a word of English, and he failed the first two quarters of his high school classes.

With the help of a teacher, Franklin caught up and began doing well in school, eventually earning his degree and a full-ride scholarship to study engineering. He was elated—until his scholarship was unexpectedly rescinded. It turned out that he wasn't eligible for financial aid because he wasn't a US citizen. When Franklin's former teachers found out what had happened, they started a petition, and the state legislature decided to award Franklin a one-year scholarship and reduced tuition.

> He would have to take out loans and work to pay his way through school, but Franklin was *finally* on his way to making his dreams come true.

He graduated college, earning a bachelor of science in mechanical engineering. But when the National Aeronautics and Space Administration (NASA) suspended its space program, Franklin was disappointed all over again. He decided to bide his time and hope his fortune would turn, enrolling at the Massachusetts Institute of Technology (MIT) to study physics and nuclear energy while he waited.

In 1977, Franklin earned his PhD in applied plasma physics and fusion technology. The same year, NASA relaunched its space program and put out a call for astronauts. Franklin enthusiastically applied—and was selected! His dream of seeing the stars from the window of a spaceship would come true!

> In 1986, Franklin became the first Latine astronaut to go to space. He made a total of seven flights, logging over 1,500 hours in space.

He also served as director of the Space Propulsion Laboratory and as a visiting scientist at MIT. In 2002, he participated in three space walks to repair the robotic arm of the International Space Station. Three years later, after more than twenty years living out his dream at NASA, he finally retired from space travel.

> But Franklin wasn't done yet—he decided to start his own rocket company!

Ad Astra Rocket Company's mission was to help create a more sustainable future for all of humanity. By using plasma—a type of gas that conducts electricity—it was able to develop new rocket technology that would, one day, revolutionize the space industry by making it easier for spacecraft to travel longer distances.

In 2012, Franklin was inducted into NASA's US Astronaut Hall of Fame, a testament to his extraordinary contributions to the field of space technology. His enduring optimism and refusal to give up has left future spacefarers a powerful message: With perseverance and determination, no dream is too big to accomplish.

SYLVIA RIVERA

{ Gay Liberation and Transgender Rights Activist
1951–2002
Heritage: Puerto Rican and Venezuelan }

SYLVIA RIVERA never shied away from fighting to be who she was. Even when faced with crushing hardship, she never lost her sense of identity. Orphaned before she was three, Sylvia was raised by her abuela, who often punished her for refusing to conform to societal gender norms.

> Though Sylvia was assigned male at birth, in her heart, she *knew* she was a girl.

She liked nothing more than to try on her abuela's dresses and experiment with her makeup. But Sylvia's strict abuela deemed such interests unacceptable, and she was not the only one who refused to accept Sylvia's transgender identity. When Sylvia wore makeup to school, the other kids picked on her and called her names.

By the time she was eleven, she felt like such an outcast that she left home and dropped out of school. She was forced to live on the streets, where she faced more abuse and violence. But she also made lifelong friends—people like Marsha P. Johnson, a Black transgender woman—who were accepting of Sylvia just the way she was.

Marsha was part of a community of drag queens and trans people who, like Sylvia, had been largely rejected by society. They welcomed Sylvia warmly and gave her a much-needed sense of family.

> Together, the community helped one another survive in a world that felt threatened by their existence.

Inspired by the activism of the gay rights groups of New York City, Sylvia began participating in the movements for wider social change that pervaded the 1960s.

When she was just seventeen, Sylvia was part of the Stonewall uprisings, throwing Molotov cocktails at police raiding a gay bar at the Stonewall Inn in Manhattan. This incident—a response to police corruption and years of targeted persecution—was the first spark in a nationwide movement to defend the rights of the LGBTQ+ community.

> It inspired Sylvia to become as vocal as she could about the challenges faced by transgender people.

She became active in the Gay Liberation Front and the Gay Activists Alliance, and in 1970, alongside Marsha, Sylvia founded her own political organization, STAR (Street Transvestite* Action Revolutionaries).

Sylvia worked tirelessly with these organizations to push for antidiscrimination legislation, going so far as to climb the walls of New York City Hall to interrupt a closed-door meeting. Together with Marsha, she raised funds to help transgender youth who—like Sylvia and so many of her friends—found themselves facing homelessness, incarceration, and violence. But she often clashed with the white, middle-class organizers who dominated the gay rights movement, feeling that they were more interested in assimilation than in helping the most vulnerable members of the LGBTQ+ community. Sylvia was vocal in her criticisms and unwavering in her fight for inclusivity. In 1973, she gave an impassioned speech at one of the United States' first gay pride rallies, in which she voiced her sense of betrayal and outrage at being forbidden to speak. When Sylvia learned that the legislation she had worked so hard for ended up excluding the transgender community, she left the movement—and activism altogether—for nearly twenty years.

It wasn't until the mid-1990s that Sylvia returned to the cause, amid national debate about issues such as marriage equality and the right for LGBTQ+ people to serve in the military.

> She renewed her push for inclusion, speaking up for transgender rights once again and reviving STAR in an effort to make the ongoing struggles of the trans community more public.

In 2002—the year of Sylvia's death—the Sylvia Rivera Law Project was founded, providing unprecedented legal protections and leadership opportunities for trans and gender-fluid people.

Sylvia's work transformed the gay rights movement, pushing it to be more inclusive and more visionary. Through her unwavering determination for the transgender community to be seen and heard, she opened new doors and began paving a path toward *true* inclusivity.

---

*The term *transvestite* is now outdated and considered derogatory by many but was a commonly used term within the LGBTQ+ community at the time.

SONIA SOTOMAYOR

{ **Supreme Court Justice**
1954–
Heritage: Puerto Rican }

SONIA SOTOMAYOR had an early fascination with the principle of *justice*: the idea that everyone has a right to be treated fairly under the law. She grew up watching episodes of *Perry Mason*, a television show about a lawyer who defended falsely accused people, and was moved by how one person—a judge—could have such an impact on people's lives.

> Since judges were the ones who saw justice done, Sonia made up her mind, then and there: She, too, would become a judge so she could change the world for the better.

There were no lawyers or judges in the Bronx housing projects where Sonia lived, but her mother encouraged her dreams and supported her studies however possible. Sonia worked hard and excelled academically, graduating from high school in 1972 at the top of her class. She earned a scholarship to Princeton University, where she graduated with the highest honors, and went on to enroll in Yale Law School—one step closer to realizing her dreams.

Though Sonia sometimes felt out of place in the Ivy League, where most of her classmates knew nothing of the culture she had grown up in, she found a sense of community in student-run groups like Accion Puertorriqueña (Puerto Rican Action).

> Sonia used her voice to defend what she believed in—even in the face of those with more power.

On one occasion, she spoke out against what she believed were the discriminatory hiring practices of her undergraduate institution. Few students would dare to oppose such a powerful administration. But Sonia was fearless when it came to matters of justice.

Upon earning her law degree in 1979, Sonia began her career as an assistant district attorney. She took a position in Manhattan, where she was responsible for prosecuting cases of robbery, murder, and police brutality. Though young, she held her own in the courtroom, earning a reputation as an imposing prosecutor who would not be intimidated. When Sonia was thirty, she moved into private practice and was quickly made a partner at a commercial firm.

While sharpening her skills as a litigator, Sonia ventured into pro bono work, donating her services to organizations such as the Puerto Rican Legal Defense and Education Fund. It was this work—the work that spoke to Sonia's tireless commitment to real justice—that caught the attention of Senators Ted Kennedy and Daniel Patrick Moynihan. On their recommendation, President George H. W. Bush appointed her to the US District Court in 1992.

> Sonia was unanimously confirmed by the Senate, becoming the youngest of all the judges in the court.

She had achieved her lifelong dream of presiding over justice as a judge! But her work was only just beginning. There was still much to do.

On Sonia's forty-third birthday, President Bill Clinton nominated her to the US Court of Appeals Second Circuit. And in 2009, Sonia became the first Latina justice ever appointed to the US Supreme Court! She has worked fearlessly for justice in every ruling, defending protections for historically marginalized communities; upholding affirmative action programs that systematize equity in hiring and education; and prioritizing affordable health care and the right to marriage for all people. She has brought more experience to her seat than any justice in one hundred years!

> Sonia became known as the People's Justice for her unapologetic defense of constitutional liberties and for helping maintain a true moral compass in a court often swayed by politics.

She has never abandoned her early dedication to justice for all people, regardless of how much money they have or where they come from. Though the US government changes hands, often shifting the landscape of political discourse, Sonia continues to work tirelessly to remain a guardian of liberty for *all* American people.

MARÍA ELENA SALINAS

{ Journalist and News Anchor
1954–
Heritage: Mexican }

MARÍA ELENA SALINAS grew up in a humble home in Los Angeles. Though it was sometimes difficult to make ends meet, her parents did their best to meet every challenge with optimism. María Elena's mother, a seamstress, believed in working hard and focusing on the positive. And her father, a well-educated former priest, always maintained a sense of charity.

When María Elena was young, there were very few television stations in the United States that broadcast the news in Spanish. And the stations that *did* exist were small and underfunded, which meant there was virtually no media representing Latin American communities or informing them about current events.

Though María Elena never dreamed that she would one day become a reporter, in her heart she knew that *someone* had to advocate for her community.

As a child, María Elena nursed dreams of working with clothing like her mother. She enrolled in community college for two years to pursue this early ambition, but life would soon steer her back toward her penchant for advocacy. In 1979, María Elena took a job as a DJ as a stepping stone into radio marketing. She played music on air—but she also had a talent for reading the news, which soon led to other opportunities.

It was not long before María Elena was offered the job as host of a public affairs program called *Los Ángeles Ahora* for Channel 34, a local Spanish-language TV station.

Though it took her away from her marketing ambitions, she was intrigued. She knew it would take a lot of hard work to learn to be a reporter and anchor, but maybe María Elena could be the one to *finally* amplify her community's voice!

María Elena seized this new challenge with the optimism and sense of mission her parents had raised her with. She went back to school, taking courses in broadcast journalism at the University of California, Los Angeles, to hone her skills. Soon, she was offered the position of network anchor for the national late-night news show on Channel 34. Univision (the United States' largest Spanish-language network) then asked María to coanchor the evening news with a man named Jorge Ramos. Together, they were a magnetic duo, drawing in scores of late-night viewers.

Before long, María Elena became known as one of the most influential Latina personalities in television!

María Elena worked for Univision for thirty-seven years, covering major world events from natural disasters to wars to elections. She was one of the first woman reporters to cover the Iraq War from the ground, and in 2007, she made history as the cohost of the first US presidential election forums ever broadcast on a Spanish-language network. During her decades-long career, María Elena interviewed countless powerful figures: prime ministers, dictators, rebel leaders, and every US president since Jimmy Carter.

She became an industry icon and one of the most recognizable female anchors on TV, making it her personal mission to amplify the voices of Latin American communities like the one she grew up in.

In addition to using her platform to advocate for issues like immigration reform, María Elena provided scholarships to help aspiring Latine journalists break into, and succeed in, the industry. She earned countless honors for her work in television, radio, and print news media, including several Emmys, a Peabody, and a Walter Cronkite Award. María Elena took the lessons of her childhood—lessons of hard work, positivity, and compassion—and used them to build a career with lasting impact, one that helped shape the Spanish-language news media into the powerful industry it is today.

MARICEL PRESILLA

Chef, Writer, and Historian
1952–
Heritage: Cuban

A love of food was in **MARICEL PRESILLA**'s DNA. Descended from a line of artists, teachers, and cacao farmers who delighted in cooking, she learned everything from her family—from raising livestock to creating savory meals.

> Food was the thing that brought them all together every day.

They had long, formal lunches each afternoon in Cuba, until Fidel Castro's revolution disrupted the life they were used to. Where once they had enjoyed bountiful meals, they now found themselves unable to afford much more than rice, small portions of meat, and the occasional mango. Maricel had to cross a river just to buy a single jug of milk!

In 1970, when Maricel was in her early twenties, her family immigrated to Miami to escape Cuba. They arrived empty-handed, unable to take anything from their former lives with them on their journey.

> Life away from home was bittersweet, but Maricel made the most of the experience.

She enrolled in college as a history major and earned money teaching Spanish in her spare time. Whenever she could, Maricel read cookbooks, re-creating recipes—and happy memories—from her childhood.

The next year, 1971, Maricel married. A year later, she followed her husband to Spain, where she enrolled as a student of medieval history at a local university. But while doing research at a church, instead of taking notes on the historical figures buried at the site, she found herself more curious about the food and liquor that had once been consumed there. As she traveled throughout Latin America, trying new dishes (pasteles from Puerto Rico, pizza from Argentina, lizard omelets from Peru), she found herself drawn as much to the stories behind the recipes as to the food itself.

Food held memories, she knew, serving as a window into the identities of individuals and entire communities and cultures.

Maricel's insatiable curiosity about the culture of food yielded notebooks full of recipes and stories and eventually brought her to a Manhattan restaurant called the Ballroom, where she began training as a chef. Though she continued her studies in history and even earned her doctorate in 1989, her growing expertise as a chef led to work as a food consultant and as a writer for magazines.

It was during this time that she realized her life's work really was food!

Through food, Maricel could finally begin to share her enthusiasm, creativity, and knowledge with the world.

It was not long before Maricel was introduced to Maria Guarnaschelli, an editor who happened to be looking for a book about Latin American cuisine. Maricel and Maria decided it was fate that they work together. But Maricel didn't want it to be just *any* book—her book would be the ultimate authority on Latin cooking! Over many decades, visiting more than twenty countries throughout Latin America, Maricel continued to fill her endless travel notebooks with recipes and inspiration—for example, turkey thighs in a smoky broth flavored with toasted cacao nibs, inspired by the residue found on cooking vessels unearthed at Maya archaeological sites! In 2012, her epic tome—*Gran Cocina Latina: The Food of Latin America*—was published to great acclaim, indeed becoming known as the ultimate authority on Latin American cooking and winning several awards. That same year, Maricel was named Best Chef by the James Beard Foundation—she was the first Latina in the organization's history to receive this distinction! Her book became the inspiration for two restaurants and a Latin food market, which she opened with her business partner, Clara Chaumont.

Maricel's restaurants soon became community staples and popular travel destinations. But the accomplishment Maricel prized most of all was an invitation to cook for the president of the United States! Under the Obama administration, the White House opened its doors to the first annual Fiesta Latina, a culinary celebration of Latin American culture. Maricel delighted in serving everything from Argentinean beef empanadas to Cuban roast pork canapés. She used an assortment of traditional spices in every dish (including the hot chocolate!) and even placed colorful peppers instead of flowers in her centerpieces.

Maricel's books and recipes have given readers a glimpse into the varied and vibrant cultural identities of many different Latin American countries.

Her passion for food has transformed what the world knows about Latin American cooking while also preserving traditional practices once only handed down orally and in danger of being forgotten.

Food, to Maricel, is not only a reflection of the soul of Latine history and tradition but also a lasting source of comfort, connection, and her fondest memories of home.

SANDRA CISNEROS

{ Writer
1954–
Heritage: Mexican }

SANDRA CISNEROS grew up in a house that hummed with the sounds of nine people. The only girl among six other children, she often felt unheard. Though Sandra was born in Chicago, her family moved many times, leaving her feeling uprooted—and caught between two cultures, not always sure which one she belonged to. Her parents, like Sandra's grandparents before them, had immigrated to the United States from Mexico, and her family traveled frequently between the two countries to visit relatives.

Life was chaotic—even at school, from which Sandra was often absent.

 But she found solace in one special place: the library, her refuge. The library was *quiet*, making it the perfect place for her imagination to roam free.

Sandra loved to sit in the silence, reading books or daydreaming quietly. When she was ten, she found a new way to combat her loneliness—she wrote her first poem. It didn't sound like anyone else. It sounded like *her*. Maybe writing was how Sandra could make her voice heard.

After graduating from high school, Sandra did something her family would have never imagined: She decided to go to college. She enrolled at Loyola University, where she received a bachelor's degree in English, then continued her studies at the University of Iowa's Writers' Workshop. But the Writers' Workshop was not everything she had hoped it would be. Sandra struggled with feelings of alienation—especially because the literature she was studying centered on the experiences of white Americans, not on people like her.

 Still, she would not be deterred from her dream of becoming a writer.

In 1980, just two years after earning her master's degree, Sandra published *Bad Boys*, her first book of poetry. Two years later, she won a National Endowment for the Arts Fellowship. She used the money to travel to Europe, where she wrote her first novel. *The House on Mango Street*, a story loosely based on her own experiences as a young girl, was published to international acclaim. Sandra finally had a sense of purpose—and a way to share her voice with others!

Though Sandra's first novel was received well, earning her an American Book Award, she was still unable to make a living as an author. She struggled with feelings of sadness, unsure whether she had made the right career choice.

 But Sandra loved writing, and she couldn't abandon her passion so easily. She channeled her anxieties into words, using writing to work through her struggles.

Sandra went on to publish several more books to critical acclaim, and after winning the PEN/Nabokov Award for Achievement in International Literature in 2019, she was able to buy a house with her earnings. *The House on Mango Street* went on to sell more than six million copies, was translated into more than twenty languages, and became required reading at schools all over the United States.

In 2016, Sandra was awarded the National Medal of Arts by President Barack Obama for her vast contributions to American literature.

Though there had been moments when she thought she would give up, she persevered in pursuing her passion.

By remaining true to herself and writing in a style all her own, Sandra not only found a way to feel heard but also helped generations of readers find themselves within the pages of her stories.

MARI CARMEN RAMÍREZ

Museum Curator
1955–
Heritage: Puerto Rican

MARI CARMEN RAMÍREZ grew up fiercely proud of her Puerto Rican identity. She always loved the arts, but she did *not* love how the art world largely ignored Latine artists. While critics and scholars lauded a select few, they overlooked the talents of many working throughout Latin America in the modern day. Mari hailed from a family of scholars and artists who encouraged her interest. But with museums so scarce on the island, she was forced to find other ways to study. She learned what she could from the writings and lectures of prominent Puerto Rican scholars before enrolling at the University of Puerto Rico and, later, at the University of Chicago.

As a doctoral candidate in art history, Mari was keen to study Latin American art, but she was quickly disappointed by the lack of existing scholarship. Many still viewed Latin American art as inferior to Western art, dismissing it as "exotic" and largely ignoring the diverse catalog of contemporary Latine creators.

Mari, determined to champion change, accepted a position at the art museum at the University of Texas at Austin just before completing her dissertation in 1988, becoming the first curator of Latin American art in the United States and seizing her chance to reform the art world from within.

She began organizing shows the likes of which no one in the country had seen before, displaying abstract Latine art in place of the Western art everyone was used to and earning herself a name among scholars while growing the museum's reputation.

After twelve years curating in Austin, Mari became the first director of the Museum of Fine Arts, Houston, International Center for the Arts of the Americas. Even though most of Houston's population came from Latine backgrounds, Latine artists were woefully underrepresented within the museum's collection. Mari was intent on changing that. In 2004, she rose to prominence with a groundbreaking exhibition called *Inverted Utopias*.

The show featured avant-garde Latin American artists whose work had rarely been displayed in the United States, prompting *Time* magazine to name Mari one of 2005's Most Influential Hispanics in America.

Mari made frequent trips to Latin America to scout undiscovered talent, unearthing astonishing new works of art in hidden corners—and even underneath beds! She showcased the talents of artists such as Gego (a German-born Venezuelan sculptor) and Joaquín Torres-García (an Uruguayan artist who combined pre-Columbian themes with modernism). And in 2012, she organized an effort to collect, archive, and disseminate thousands of important art documents that would radically contribute to the scholarship of Latine art.

Though much work remains to be done, Mari's groundbreaking efforts as a curator have helped shift the way Latine artists are perceived. By assembling some of the largest and most impressive collections of Latine art the world has ever seen, Mari has paved the way for future generations of scholars and artists to find representation within a diversified artistic landscape.

ELLEN OCHOA

{ Astronaut
1958–
Heritage: Mexican }

ELLEN OCHOA's mother taught her to reach for the stars—that with hard work and study, *anything* was possible. Ellen loved to learn, but it was hard to choose just one focus! She liked math and science and playing the flute, and she excelled at almost everything she tried. After graduating as valedictorian of her high school class, she considered studying music in college but, instead, decided to chase her curiosity about the natural world and pursue physics. As a graduate student, she studied optics—the behavior and characteristics of light—and even patented some of her work before completing her doctorate.

> There was no question that Ellen was on her way to a great career, and in 1985, she decided to apply to the coveted space program at the National Aeronautics and Space Administration (NASA).

Just two years earlier, Sally Ride had made history as the first woman astronaut. Ellen saw no reason why she couldn't follow in Sally's footsteps.

In 1990, Ellen was accepted into NASA's rigorous astronaut training program. The program was *tough*, putting trainees through a multitude of mental and physical challenges. Ellen took rigorous courses and exams in many different disciplines, including space sciences, astronomy, geology, oceanography, meteorology, first aid, survival techniques, and space shuttle design. She began her work for NASA as a flight software specialist in robotics development and, a short two years later, was unexpectedly chosen for her very first space mission!

> In 1993, Ellen joined the STS-56 mission of the space shuttle *Discovery*, making history as the first Latina to fly in space!

She enjoyed working with her crewmates to study the sun and its effects on Earth's atmosphere. And of course, Ellen *loved* the view from the shuttle. There was nothing else like it.

Ellen returned to space three more times, continuing the work she had started on *Discovery* while also embarking on brand-new missions. In 1999, she and her colleagues were the first to dock aboard the International Space Station (ISS), carrying much-needed supplies for the astronauts who would soon be living there full time. On one of her missions, Ellen delighted her crewmates with a fifteen-minute concert, playing songs on her flute while she floated weightlessly in orbit around the Earth. Though she loved being an astronaut, Ellen retired from space travel in 2007, continuing her work on the ground as deputy director for the Johnson Space Center in Houston. She made history again as the first Latina woman—and second woman overall—to accept the position, and she was soon elevated to the role of director.

> In 2017, Ellen was inducted into the US Astronaut Hall of Fame, having made countless contributions to the field of space exploration.

The following year, she retired from her many years of service at the Johnson Space Center and became vice chair of the National Science Board, which runs the National Science Foundation. Having logged nearly one thousand hours in space and excelled in all aspects of her work, Ellen has received many prestigious awards, including NASA's Distinguished Service Medal. A fierce advocate of the power of education, she has given 150 talks during her decades-long career, encouraging students to reach for the stars—and beyond! By staying curious, studying hard, and believing in herself, Ellen broke many barriers, unveiling a *universe* of limitless potential for future Latine heroes.

RIGOBERTA MENCHÚ TUM

Activist
1959–
Heritage: Guatemalan

RIGOBERTA MENCHÚ TUM was born a descendant of the Maya, a once highly advanced and prosperous civilization, but she grew up in poverty and under extreme oppression. Rigoberta and her family picked cotton in the fields of large landowners, where peasant workers often suffered from malnutrition and were exposed to dangerous fungicides. Though her parents had never learned to read or write, they were respected leaders within their community. Her mother was a midwife who tended to the sick, and her father was the founder of the Peasant Unity Committee.

Inspired by her parents, Rigoberta joined the women's rights movement in Guatemala, speaking out about the struggles of Indigenous women when she was a teen. But her family suffered a heavy price for their activism. They were targeted by the Guatemalan government, which routinely used violence to shut down peaceful protests.

> Her parents and two of her brothers were eventually killed by the Guatemalan military, and Rigoberta, devastated by the sudden loss of her family, vowed to fight even harder for the causes they believed in.

She deepened her activism, teaching herself Spanish and other Mayan languages in addition to Quiché, participating in public marches and rallies, and teaching the women of her community how to build encampments and defend themselves against military offensives.

In 1981, in the face of persistent death threats, Rigoberta was forced to flee the country. She relocated to Mexico, where she continued to stand against the exploitation and genocide of Indigenous peoples in Guatemala.

> Rigoberta brought their struggles to the international stage, speaking openly to the United Nations about the mistreatment of her people.

She went on to help create the United Representation of the Guatemalan Opposition, an organization comprising thousands of exiled Maya fighting for Indigenous rights in Mexico. The Guatemalan government responded with slander and dangerous threats. But when Rigoberta published her life story in a book entitled *I, Rigoberta Menchú*, her audience only grew larger. The book received international acclaim and brought global attention to the plight of the Maya in Guatemala. Rigoberta would not be swayed from her cause—she would fight for her people to the end.

> In 1992, Rigoberta was awarded the Nobel Peace Prize for her commitment to social justice.

She used the prize money to found the Rigoberta Menchú Tum Foundation, an advocacy organization for Indigenous populations. The following year, 1993, was declared the International Year for the World's Indigenous People by the United Nations, in large part thanks to Rigoberta's advocacy and influence. Rigoberta, with her tireless courage and activism, has shone a light on the struggles of Indigenous peoples and helped usher in an era of recognition *and* reparation.

ISABEL TOLEDO

Fashion Designer
1960–2019
Heritage: Cuban

ISABEL TOLEDO wanted to be a fashion designer from the time she was eight, but she didn't just want to make clothes—she wanted *her* designs to be wearable art! She had long been intrigued by her grandmother's sewing machine, and she was thrilled when a babysitter finally taught her how to use it. She loved the feel of fabric beneath her fingers and the way she was able to shape it stitch by stitch.

When Isabel's family moved to New Jersey, she brought her passion with her, along with the distinctive sense of fashion she had grown up with in Cuba.

> Sporting asymmetrical haircuts and bold makeup, Isabel stood out in school as the girl with *style*.

She quickly caught the eye of Ruben Toledo, a boy in her Spanish class who, like her, was an artist. It wasn't long before they embarked on a lifelong partnership together.

After graduating from high school, Isabel enrolled at the Fashion Institute of Technology and, later, at the Parsons School of Design, but she never finished a degree program. She was less interested in learning by reading than she was in learning by

doing. So, she left school when she was nineteen to intern at the Costume Institute at the Metropolitan Museum of Art.

 She began designing clothes by experimenting with fabric, letting her imagination flow freely.

Unlike other designers, Isabel was able to visualize three-dimensional designs without the help of a computer. While others needed specialized technology to create models of their designs, Isabel was thought of by many as a genius for being able to do in her head what a computer could do.

In 1984, Isabel and Ruben married—and the following year, Isabel showed her first collection at New York Fashion Week! Her pieces were suddenly in high demand with major stores such as Barneys, Colette, and Joyce, earning her a following in fashion hubs like New York, Paris, and Tokyo.

She quickly became known as a "designer's designer," at once meticulous and utterly original.

And unlike most other designers, she made her clothing to fit people of all sizes and budgets.

Isabel's insistence on doing things her own way did not come without challenges. She had difficulties with financial investors despite her undeniable talent. But Isabel cared less about wealth and celebrity than she did about honoring her craft, remaining humble no matter how highly her work was praised. By the '90s, she had rejected the runway altogether, preferring to exhibit her designs in museums, where craftsmanship was valued above profit and Isabel's creations could be admired for what they truly were—works of art. But despite her aversion to stardom, fame found Isabel anyway when she designed an inaugural dress for First Lady Michelle Obama in 2009. The shift dress and matching overcoat were unlike anything ever worn for the historic event, replacing the traditional conservative palette with a "hopeful" lemongrass-colored fabric. Isabel's design wowed the world, catapulting her to celebrity status and inspiring countless young designers to come.

Isabel used her newfound platform to support up-and-coming immigrant designers and to continue promoting inclusive fashion by making clothing for women of all shapes, sizes, and income levels.

She received many honors for her groundbreaking work, including the Cooper Hewitt Museum's prestigious National Design Award—and she was even nominated for a Tony Award in costume design for the Broadway musical *After Midnight*. When Isabel died in 2019, the entire fashion world mourned the loss of a true original. Isabel will be remembered for her visionary work, at once unique and universal—for creating designs that were both functional and beautiful pieces of art.

JEAN-MICHEL BASQUIAT

{ Artist
1960–1988
Heritage: Haitian and Puerto Rican }

People often said that **JEAN-MICHEL BASQUIAT** came into the world fully formed. Born with the soul of an artist, he burned so bright and brilliant that it was impossible to ignore his light. His mother, noting Jean-Michel's innate talents, encouraged him to learn to draw and took him to art exhibitions throughout New York City. By the age of six, he was enrolled as a junior member at the Brooklyn Museum. He knew without a doubt that, someday, he would become an artist.

But the path to success wasn't easy for Jean-Michel, even when he was young. His parents divorced when he was seven years old, and he and his siblings were sent to live with their strict father. Around the same time, Jean-Michel was hit by a car while playing with friends in the street and underwent surgery to remove part of his abdomen.

During his recovery, his mother gave him a copy of *Gray's Anatomy*, an illustrated book about the human body that ignited Jean-Michel's imagination.

The illustrations had such an impact on him that they would later influence his own art. But for young Jean-Michel, there were still more trials to come.

When Jean-Michel was eleven years old, his mother was admitted to a hospital for help with mental health issues. He had difficulty concentrating in school, spending most of his time drawing instead of studying. As a teenager, Jean-Michel ran away more than once to escape a troubled home life. Eventually, he dropped out of high school and left home for good. He relied on the kindness of friends, who loaned him their couches and floors for the night, and scraped together money for food by selling postcards and searching for change on the ground.

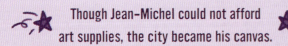

Though Jean-Michel could not afford art supplies, the city became his canvas.

He painted on windows, walls, and doors—on anything he could find. He and a friend began spray-painting the name SAMO (a cartoon character he created for a comic with schoolmates) on trains and buildings. The enigmatic name, accompanied by antiestablishment phrases and images, began to appear everywhere, leaving thousands of people hungry to know more about the artist behind them. The intrigue surrounding his work quickly grew, garnering the attention of counterculture media. Jean-Michel began frequenting clubs on the Lower East Side, where he mingled with up-and-coming artists and musicians. Slowly, opportunities arose to show his art in professional circles through these new connections. And in 1980, he received his first big break when his work was included in the historic *Times Square Show*.

In 1981, Jean-Michel was featured in an *Artforum* article entitled "The Radiant Child," catapulting him to fame and establishing him as a rising star within the art world. The following year, his work was showcased in six solo exhibitions around the globe.

He made history, at age twenty-one, as the youngest artist ever to be featured at the prestigious *Documenta* art show in Kassel, Germany.

Jean-Michel was now selling his paintings for thousands of dollars. He became a household name, embraced and celebrated by icons such as Madonna and Andy Warhol.

Both abstract and profoundly modern, Jean-Michel's art was unlike anything seen before. While most were enthralled by his frenzied sketches, some within the establishment were critical. They cast him aside for being young, for being Black, and for lacking formal training. However, whether his critics liked it or not, there was no denying that Jean-Michel was a force within the art world.

Though Jean-Michel had made his dreams come true through his talent, tireless work, and fierce determination, the pressures he faced as a young overnight success eventually took their toll. He struggled with addiction, which led to his accidental death at the age of twenty-seven. But his acclaim continued to grow, influencing countless other artists, filmmakers, and musicians. His work was known all around the world, appearing everywhere from T-shirts to galleries to private collections. Though his light was extinguished far too soon, Jean-Michel's brilliance still shone brightly long after his death, igniting a renaissance of raw expression in the art world—and inspiring new generations.

MÓNICA PONCE DE LEÓN

{ Architect
1965–
Heritage: Venezuelan }

MÓNICA PONCE DE LEÓN grew up in Caracas, Venezuela, surrounded by modernist architecture whose emphasis on cutting-edge technology delighted and inspired her. Buildings were not just walls and roofs—they defined their communities!

> They spoke volumes about how the people who used them, and those who built them, viewed the world.

Mónica knew that when she grew up, this was how *she* wanted to change the world—by making new technologies for building design that would be accessible to everyone and environmentally friendly.

Mónica moved to the United States with her family just after she graduated from high school, earning first a bachelor's degree from the University of Miami and then a master's degree in urban design from Harvard University. She finished school at a time when the building industry was undergoing radical change: While people had once used power tools for construction, new robotic technologies were quickly emerging.

Right away, Mónica saw how important these technological advances could be in promoting equity.

> In an industry where "custom-made" buildings had only been available to the very wealthy, new technologies could help make their construction more affordable.

As she began her work in higher education, she insisted on bringing innovation into her classroom, experimenting with new tools that people weren't even talking about yet.

As a professor and the dean of the Princeton University School of Architecture, and as the owner of her own architecture and design studio, Mónica now had the platform to create change. She used her experiences and expertise to speak out about the rigid practices that kept the industry from diversifying, such as requiring practical training and expensive licenses that were mostly available to only white males. As the first female dean of the Princeton University School of Architecture, Mónica increased the number of Black tenured and tenure-track professors from 0 percent to 12 percent and urged the institution to do the same for admissions, hoping the numbers could improve even further year over year.

> Mónica also made waves with her innovative approach to architecture. Her buildings were heralded for their forward-thinking design and their focus on cutting-edge technologies.

She pioneered the application of robotics in architecture, which she used to design modernistic buildings, and created some of the first sustainable buildings, such as Helios House—an entirely green gas station built in Los Angeles with a drought-resistant roof made from recycled materials.

Mónica is an undeniable force within the architecture industry, and her work has influenced the future of architecture for generations of academics and designers. She has authored many papers and won several awards for her contributions to the field, including induction into the National Academy of Design. And in 2007, she became the first Latina ever to receive the Cooper Hewitt National Design Award in Architecture!

> Both Mónica's buildings *and* her voice within the halls of academia have been instrumental in giving the world a glorious glimpse of what is possible. Not only can buildings be functional and beautiful works of art, but they can also reflect the moral character of a society striving to do better.

MÁXIMA ACUÑA DE CHAUPE

{ Activist
1970–
Heritage: Peruvian }

MÁXIMA ACUÑA DE CHAUPE was born in the mountainous highlands of Peru, where money was scarce and people depended on the land for survival.

> Her family could not afford toys, and they didn't have the resources to send her to school, so Máxima spent her childhood helping them in the fields.

She did chores around the house and cared for her hearing-impaired brother, using her spare time to make clothes from handwoven fabric. Máxima and her mother would collect local plants to dye the fabric they made, then transform the fabric into art they could sell at the market.

Máxima entered into an arranged marriage when she was fourteen years old. She had four children and joined her husband laboring on other people's farms. They lived simply, raising animals and produce they could eat or sell for income. After a time, the family had saved enough money to buy their own land.

> Determined that her children would not have to work as hard as she had, Máxima sent them to school.

Together, the family lived a happy life surrounded by nature's beauty. But Máxima's joy was disrupted by an unwelcome intrusion when, in 2011, the mining industry came knocking on her door.

Newmont, one of the world's largest mining companies, had plans to build an open-pit gold mine, and Máxima's family was right in the middle of its chosen location. The Conga mine would destroy the mountains, the fields, and the surrounding lakes, putting Máxima and her entire community in peril. Máxima turned down the company's offer to buy her land. But Newmont was used to getting its way, and it would not take no for an answer. The company came back with a team of police who served Máxima a notice of eviction. In protest, she rushed to show them the title to her land. But in response, the police destroyed her home.

Máxima went to the local authorities, but they dismissed her complaints, leaving the family to defend itself against a mounting corporate army. When Newmont returned, it intensified its response, beating Máxima and her daughter unconscious.

The company stole the family's food and belongings, leaving them with nothing to live on.

> Desperate, Máxima sought the help of a nonprofit organization called GRUFIDES, which assisted local families in their fight against the mining company.

GRUFIDES agreed to provide legal representation and push back against Newmont's ruthless harassment. The mining company responded by suing Máxima on false allegations, accusing her family of squatting illegally on their own parcel of land. Against all logic, the courts sided with Newmont and found Máxima guilty, sentencing her to jail time and fining her an exorbitant sum of money.

Máxima's family was served with an order of eviction and given thirty days to leave. But Máxima refused to give up, enlisting the help of a legal nonprofit and collecting documents proving her legitimate claim to the land.

> The Peruvian courts eventually overturned her conviction, and, in 2016, Máxima was awarded the Goldman Environmental Prize for her courageous defense of the environment and her home.

She accepted the prestigious award by singing a song called "La Jalaqueñita," detailing the plight her community had faced at the hands of corporate greed. She dedicated the award to the many people throughout history who had died protecting their land, and she vowed to continue fighting for environmental conservation. Her moving acceptance song garnered international attention, which Máxima used to launch an effort to try her case in the United States.

Though the fight was long and hard, Máxima eventually won the right to a fair trial, granting hope not only to her own family but also to others all over the world whose rights had so long been ignored. Thanks to Máxima's courageous efforts, the voices of subsistence farmers were finally being heard. Her fight to raise awareness has encouraged people everywhere to never give up on justice.

SYLVIA POLL

{ Swimmer
1970–
Heritage: Costa Rican }

SYLVIA POLL had no reason to believe she would win an Olympic medal. No one from the small country of Costa Rica, where she had grown up, had ever won before.

> But Sylvia's coach insisted that anything was possible with hard work and the right frame of mind.

Most important of all was for Sylvia to believe she had a shot at winning—that the medal was hers for the taking.

Sylvia's parents were both German but moved to Nicaragua before Sylvia was born. When she was nine, her family moved to Costa Rica, where she and her younger sister, Claudia, joined a swimming club close to their new home. They both soon began training with the club's owner, Francisco Rivas, who became their long-term coach.

> Sylvia *loved* to swim, and her coach saw that she and her sister were gifted athletes.

He taught them to play volleyball, basketball, and water polo as a way of strengthening their abilities. Sylvia was so good at all three sports that she could have easily competed in any of them. But she was a natural at swimming—she moved like lightning through the water!

At first, Sylvia did not want to work hard. Her coach said she lacked discipline. But before long, she and her sister established a rigorous routine. They began training together for five hours every day, never missing a practice. Soon, Sylvia saw what she could do with confidence in her abilities. Even when ill or injured, she pushed on, determined to recover and become even stronger than she had been before.

When she was sixteen, Sylvia competed in the Central American and Caribbean Games against some of the best swimmers in the world. She finished with ten medals, blowing away the competition in every event and taking her first big step toward becoming a world-class athlete. Two months later, she traveled to Indianapolis to participate in the Pan American Games. Sylvia made history when she won the gold medal—the very first gold for Costa Rica! Over the course of the games, she won three golds, three silvers, and two bronze medals in various freestyle events.

> When she returned home, Sylvia was a hero, celebrated all across Central America.

Now it was time to work toward her long-held dream of competing in the Olympics.

In 1988, Sylvia traveled to Seoul, Korea, to compete in the Summer Olympics. She was slow to start in every event . . . but that was all part of her plan. Sylvia let her competitors think she had fallen behind, then used her saved strength to speed up at the very end.

> Her clever strategy paid off when she won Costa Rica's first Olympic medal *ever*!

Sylvia finished second in the 200-meter freestyle behind Heike Friedrich of then East Germany, earning a silver medal to add to her quickly growing collection.

By the end of her career, Sylvia had amassed more than six hundred medals! She was named Best Athlete in Latin America for two years running, in 1988 and 1989. Inspired by her older sister, Claudia traveled to the Olympics to compete in 1996, where she won Costa Rica's first gold medal—historic in its own right! Sylvia and her sister did what many had doubted was possible, proving that athletes from even the smallest countries can achieve *mighty* success on a global scale.

BERTA CÁCERES

{ Activist
1971–2016
Heritage: Honduran }

BERTA CÁCERES was raised with the conviction that it is important to fight for others. When she was a child, Berta's home was a sanctuary to those seeking refuge from poverty and injustice. Her mother, Austra, was an activist and midwife who provided medical care for displaced Salvadoran immigrants and Indigenous peoples underserved by the Honduran government. Austra didn't flinch from the bigger, important fights—she even ran for political office!—so it was no surprise when Berta followed in her mother's footsteps and began to organize for change herself.

> **In 1993, Berta cofounded the Council of Popular and Indigenous Organizations of Honduras (COPINH), a political organization aimed at responding to the chronic neglect and mistreatment of Indigenous populations in Honduras.**

Not only did Indigenous communities face poverty and a lack of medical care, infrastructure, churches, and schools, but they were also under attack by the logging and mining industries. In 2006, Berta was approached by Lenca people from the Rio Blanco community who were alarmed by the sudden, unexplained influx of construction equipment and machinery invading their town. There had been no notice from the government of any construction, as required by law. What could this development mean, and who could stop it?

Berta soon discovered that a Honduran company named Desarrollos Energéticos (DESA) had plans to build a dam, the construction of which would dry up a river the Lenca community considered sacred. The Lenca had long relied on the river for water, fish, and sustainable irrigation. Berta *had* to do something to stop the building of this destructive dam!

With the help of COPINH activists, Berta organized a local assembly where members of the Lenca community formally voted to stop construction. She filed complaints with the government and led peaceful protests. She even appealed to the project's funders and the Inter-American Commission on Human Rights. But her pleas were largely ignored.

> **Corporate greed held no sympathy for the rights or well-being of Indigenous peoples.**

Unwilling to concede defeat, Berta organized a peaceful road blockade, which prevented construction crews from gaining access to the building site. The protesters stood strong for over a year against militarized attacks, and construction of the dam was eventually halted as funding began to dry up.

In 2015, Berta and COPINH were awarded the Goldman Environmental Prize, recognizing their valiant efforts in protecting land rights and the environment. The receipt of such a prestigious award helped elevate Berta's cause, and it made her a pressing threat to those who would do anything to see the dam built. The following year, Berta was murdered in her own home. Just twelve days later, Nelson García—a fellow COPINH activist—was also killed. Their deaths sparked an global outcry against humanitarian abuses in Honduras and *finally* forced international backers to withdraw from building the dam. A trial ensued, and in 2018, seven men—all executives of DESA—were convicted of Berta's murder.

Though Berta's death was a tragic loss, her legacy of activism lives on in those who continue her fight for the rights of Indigenous populations all over the world.

> **By refusing to give in, Berta was able to shine a light on corporate abuses of vulnerable communities.**

She left the world with the message her mother had passed on to her: Never stand silent in the face of oppression, and *always* fight for those in need of protection.

SHAKIRA

{ Singer and Songwriter
1977–
Heritage: Colombian }

SHAKIRA grew up in a loving home, nurtured by two parents who adored her. She took belly dancing classes and sang at talent competitions, encouraged by her family to chase her every ambition.

She wrote her first song when she was eight years old and got a record deal when she was just thirteen!

But Shakira learned at an early age that not everyone was as lucky as she was. Colombia was embroiled in a decades-long political conflict that resulted in the displacement of millions of children, many in her own community. Shakira saw how the children of La Playa, an impoverished neighborhood in the city where she lived, were left to play shirtless and barefoot in the sun, without access to decent schools or housing. She vowed to herself that, when she grew up, she would do everything she could to help. She would use her good fortune to fight the injustices she saw all around her.

Shakira's success was slow to take shape; her first two albums did not sell as well as she had hoped. Determined to achieve her dream, she took the reins on the production of her third album, cowriting the songs and overseeing the recording and mixing of each track. The record—*Pies Descalzos* (*Bare Feet*)—was a blend of rock, Latin pop, and the Arabic sounds of her father's Lebanese culture, which set her apart from other pop singers and skyrocketed her to the top of the charts. One album and four years later, Shakira won her very first Grammy for Best Latin Pop Album!

Her powerful voice and belly dancing moves had made her famous throughout Latin America.

But Shakira still had one more goal to reach: to see success in the US market.

Shakira moved to Miami with her family and learned to speak and write in English. She recruited the help of Gloria Estefan, the most successful Latina singer of all time, whose husband, Emilio, became Shakira's manager and producer. And in 2001, she succeeded in releasing her first English-language album. The record—*Laundry Service*—was a hit, selling more than two hundred thousand copies in its very first week. By 2012, Shakira had sold more than ten million albums in the United States—and, incredibly, more than seventy million albums worldwide!

Over the course of her career, Shakira has won countless awards—three Grammys and fourteen Latin Grammys among them—but she began implementing her planned philanthropic efforts right away.

She donated a portion of the profits from her first commercially successful album to projects aimed at feeding and educating underserved children in Colombia. And, in 2006, she teamed up with other artists to form ALAS (Wings), a union of singers who have used their platforms to advocate for children around the world. They have organized concerts throughout Latin America, mobilizing people to fund nutrition, education, and medical care for children from less privileged backgrounds. As a Goodwill Ambassador for the United Nations Children's Fund (UNICEF), Shakira has advocated for international protections for children—and, in 2010, she was formally honored by the United Nations for her many charitable efforts.

Though she has become the highest-selling Colombian musical artist in history, Shakira has never forgotten those with whom she vowed to share her success. She has used her platform to push for change for children all over the world . . . all while igniting the stage with her electrifying dance moves and music!

ABUELAS DE PLAZA DE MAYO

Activists
Founded in 1977
Heritage: Argentinean

In 1976, the Argentine military overthrew the country's president in a series of coups designed to destabilize the current Argentine government. The military dictatorship that followed began to reorganize the country by ruthlessly waging war on its own people.

> **For the next seven years, Argentineans lived in terror as the new government kidnapped, tortured, and killed anyone it saw as a threat.**

Leftists, socialists, and activists were all taken from their families without explanation. When people disappeared, their children—some of them newborns whose mothers were killed by the government shortly after giving birth—were secretly given to families that supported the new regime. By the end of these harrowing years, nearly thirty thousand people had disappeared.

During this time, the mothers of those who were missing began desperately searching for their children.

> **They protested the actions of the new government, gathering at the Plaza de Mayo in front of the presidential palace.**

The government often retaliated with violence, but the madres would not give up. They continued their daily protests, speaking out and demanding the return of their missing children.

Many of the protesters were also grandmothers—abuelas—who had lost not just their children but their grandchildren, too. They joined the madres in a desperate search for information about their loved ones' whereabouts. The abuelas looked everywhere for their grandchildren—in courts, orphanages, and public offices. No one would give them any answers as to where the missing children had gone, but the abuelas would not give up.

As many years of searching passed, the abuelas encountered a new and puzzling problem—their grandchildren, some of whom they had never even met, would now be grown and impossible to recognize on sight. They reached out to an exiled Argentine geneticist and learned that, even if a child's parents were no longer alive, the abuelas could use their *own* DNA to determine parentage. They eagerly used this knowledge to help create a national genetic database that could reunite missing children with their birth families.

The abuelas began an information campaign, running newspaper ads and printing flyers with the aim of reaching young adults who had questions about their identities. The campaign was a success. Using the genetic database, the abuelas were able to locate 120 of their grandchildren! But they weren't done searching yet. They wanted to find *all* of their missing loved ones. They believed that every child had a right to know their birth family, and they participated in the United Nations Convention on the Rights of the Child to fight for this belief.

> **The abuelas pushed to include clauses in the treaty that would guarantee a child's right to their identity, and eventually, the Argentine Constitution was ratified to include similar language.**

They also petitioned the government to create the National Commission on the Right to Identity, which assisted adults in confirming their parentage using the National Bank of Genetic Data that the abuelas had helped create.

In 1983, the return of democracy to Argentina led to legal action against those who had perpetrated heinous war crimes against the country's people. The Trial of the Juntas saw the prosecution of nine military leaders, but only five were convicted and sentenced. In 2012, however, a new trial prosecuted fifty-four more military officers. The trial lasted five grueling years, but in the end, twenty-nine of the defendants were sentenced.

> **The verdict stood thanks to ample evidence provided by the abuelas, whose tireless activism earned them five nominations for the Nobel Peace Prize.**

Years of brutality had left painful wounds on Argentina and its people. But because of the abuelas' perseverance and enduring love, those wounds could now begin to heal.

LUIS VON AHN

{ Computer Scientist and Entrepreneur
1978–
Heritage: Guatemalan }

LUIS VON AHN was interested in computers from the time he was a little boy. When he was eight, his mother bought him a Commodore 64 computer, which was difficult to use at first because it required a knowledge of programming commands. But Luis loved nothing more than a challenge—especially when it came to technology!—and he was soon coding with ease.

Luis's parents, both doctors, spared no expense when it came to their son's education. They sent him to a private English-language school and encouraged him to pursue his dreams. But even as a boy, Luis was aware that not everyone was as fortunate as he was. Growing up in Guatemala, he saw a striking disparity in wealth among the country's citizens.

Luis felt privileged to have the freedom to learn without financial limitation. He only wished that, someday, *all* people would be given the same access to education.

When Luis was eighteen, he moved to the United States to study at Duke University, where he earned a bachelor's degree in mathematics. He went on to earn a PhD in computer science from Carnegie Mellon University, coining the term *human computation*—a way of using humans to solve problems that computers aren't capable of solving on their own—in his thesis.

Luis's work led to the creation of the Completely Automated Public Turing Test (CAPTCHA), a pioneering technology that enabled websites to differentiate between people and bots.

Though Luis and his team gave CAPTCHA to Yahoo without any thought of the money they could make from it, the revolutionary invention catapulted him to fame as a bright star in the world of technological innovation.

After his graduation, Luis joined Carnegie Mellon's computer science faculty as a professor, while also continuing his trailblazing work by developing Games with a Purpose (GWAPs). Striving for more accurate image searchability, Luis developed something called the ESP Game and licensed it to Google. The game matched two people at random and asked each of them to describe the same image in words. The more they used the same words, the more accurate a description of the image the internet gained. In 2007, Luis invented reCAPTCHA, which served a similar purpose.

This new program improved on CAPTCHA and simultaneously helped digitize books by asking people to write out words in images of physical publications.

ReCAPTCHA was instrumental in creating digital copies of books, one word at a time—up to forty million words a day! Luis figured that if people were going to spend time decoding images for security purposes, he might as well put their time to good use.

The idea that his work could serve a greater purpose set Luis on a brand-new mission. Thinking back to his childhood in Guatemala, where he'd witnessed such wealth disparity, Luis became determined to figure out how to provide free quality education to people all over the world.

In 2012, he launched Duolingo, an online learning platform that provided language instruction at no cost.

Within eight years, the company was valued at 1.5 billion dollars, but Luis's mission remained unchanged—he wanted Duolingo to remain available to all users for free. The company partnered with countries around the world to bring English instruction to their classrooms, eventually expanding to offer classes in forty-three different languages (from Spanish to Korean to High Valyrian)!

Luis's talent for technological innovation has been widely recognized, earning him many prestigious awards, including the MacArthur Fellowship (unofficially referred to as the Genius Grant). He has pioneered technology that has changed the world for the better, using his gifts in service of those who need them most.

VICTOR PINEDA

> Disability Activist
> 1978–
> Heritage: Venezuelan

From an early age, **VICTOR PINEDA'S** worldview was defined not by limitations but by imagining what was *possible*. When he was a little boy, Victor was diagnosed with spinal muscular atrophy, a condition that caused his muscles to weaken slowly. By the time he was seven years old, his legs no longer functioned. The schools of Venezuela, where Victor lived, were unequipped to take him as a student. Administrators told his mother to keep him at home, because they felt that educating him was pointless.

> **But Victor's mother would not be persuaded to give up on her son. Instead, she moved her family to the United States, where he had a chance at a future.**

When Victor was twelve years old, President George H. W. Bush signed the Americans with Disabilities Act (ADA) into law, prohibiting discrimination against people with disabilities. The ADA enabled Victor to achieve his fullest potential.

It was this idea that Victor carried with him through his studies—the idea that the world could be inclusive for people of *all* abilities. After graduating from high school, he studied at the University of California, Berkeley, and earned a dual degree in political economics and business administration. During college, Victor's lung capacity diminished, and the ventilator he had previously only needed to use at night became a daily necessity.

> **Though it wasn't easy learning to live with physical limitations, Victor refused to allow those limitations to keep him from the life he dreamed of.**

He excelled in his studies and began advocating for students with disabilities, serving as a senator in the student government and bringing back the school's defunct Disabled Students' Union. In 2006, while in graduate school, he helped draft the United Nations Convention on the Rights of Persons with Disabilities, which went into effect in 2008. Victor was the youngest government delegate to participate—and almost certainly the most ambitious.

Victor's ambitions did not end at earning a master's degree or a PhD. Empowered by his educational successes, Victor envisioned a future of inclusive cities in which people of all backgrounds and abilities would be given a chance at a fulfilling life.

> **He founded multiple organizations that pushed for new policies, planning, and urban design focused on *true* inclusivity.**

He also began teaching at UC Berkeley and continued his philanthropic efforts, teaching English language learners and advocating for disabled Latine youth who were scheduled for deportation. In 2015, President Barack Obama appointed Victor to the US Access Board, where he used his expertise to provide guidance on ADA-compliant urban designs.

Though Victor has received many awards for his work, his greatest reward has been helping people of all abilities reach their fullest potential. Refusing to resign himself to the limiting worldview of biased systems, Victor has worked tirelessly for a future in which disabled people are just as supported, valued, and encouraged as anyone else.

RUBEN VIVES

{ Journalist
1979–
Heritage: Guatemalan }

From the day he was born, **RUBEN VIVES** experienced the divide between rich and poor. His parents immigrated to the United States from Guatemala when he was just a baby, leaving Ruben behind to be raised by his grandmother until they could afford to send for him.

Once he was settled in the United States, Ruben often accompanied his mother on her rounds as a housekeeper, where he saw how well her wealthy clients lived. In contrast, the neighborhood in Echo Park where Ruben and his family lived was besieged by crime and violence. Then, when Ruben was just ten years old, his uncle was tragically killed at the hands of gang members.

> These eye-opening early experiences fundamentally shaped how Ruben viewed the world, strengthening his sense of compassion for those who, like his family, struggled due to their marginalization.

When Ruben turned seventeen, he made a terrifying discovery: The papers that granted him permission to live in the United States had long ago expired. His family was afraid that he might be deported, so they turned to a friend with influence—a columnist named Shawn Hubler who worked for the *Los Angeles Times*. Ruben and his mother had cleaned Shawn's house and become close with her family, so Shawn was glad to refer them to an immigration attorney. Once Ruben's immigration status had been remedied, Shawn invited him to apply for a job at the *Times*. He seized the opportunity, accepting an entry-level position as an editorial assistant. The job was full of menial tasks, like fetching coffee and making copies, but Ruben made a habit of also tagging along with reporters as they worked to get their stories. He helped interview victims who spoke Spanish and soon found that he liked reporting. Maybe he could be a journalist, too!

Ruben enrolled at California State University, Fullerton, and began studying journalism. His knack for storytelling soon earned him a promotion to writer of the Times Homicide Report. Ruben was diligent in his work, determined to get every detail just right. Because of his childhood experiences, he was also an exceptionally empathetic journalist, and he soon moved up the ranks to investigative reporter.

One day, Ruben and his colleague Jeff Gottlieb received a tip about financial corruption in the small town of Bell, which had a population of only 35,000 and was almost never in the news. He soon discovered that the sleepy city was embroiled in government scandal. It turned out that officials had been stealing from the town's residents for years, raising taxes on citizens—most of whom were poor and Latine—while paying themselves exorbitant salaries. The city manager was the highest-paid administrator in the entire country, with a salary almost twice that of the sitting US president! While the state of California was in financial crisis and essential services (like energy and water) were in peril, the city officials of Bell were receiving a windfall—illegally.

> Ruben and Jeff blew the story wide open, titling their series "Breach of Faith" and prompting the residents of Bell to begin protesting while the authorities investigated.

Just a few days after the story broke, Bell's city manager resigned, along with the chief of police and the assistant city manager. The entire city council was eventually replaced, and several of the city's officials were arrested and tried for corruption and fraud—including the exorbitantly paid city manager.

Thanks to his outstanding reporting and commitment to the Bell scandal's victims, Ruben was awarded the prestigious Pulitzer Prize for Public Service in 2011. He had achieved one of the greatest honors in the nation, cementing his reputation as a journalist of the highest caliber!

> But Ruben's most prized accomplishment was helping correct a grave injustice, restoring the balance of power to hardworking families just like his own.

His sense of compassion, ability to relate to marginalized communities, and refusal to get even one small detail wrong drives every story Ruben writes—making him one of the best reporters around.

CAROLINA CONTRERAS

Hair Stylist, Blogger, and Activist
1986–
Heritage: Dominican

Like many people, **CAROLINA CONTRERAS** grew up in a culture that idealized European standards of beauty: light eyes, fair skin, and straight hair that hung down your back like a waterfall. Carolina was taken to the salon for her first hair relaxer treatment when she was eight years old, and it would be nearly fifteen years before she decided it was time to love her natural hair texture.

Carolina loved everything about her Dominican roots—the food, the music, the dance. She could cook habichuelas y carne, dance bachata, and speak fluent Spanish.

> But she didn't like that so many members of her community hated their own hair—a beautiful and organic extension of their Blackness.

The idea that she needed to reject her natural hair to be beautiful felt to Carolina like a rejection of *herself*. So, after finishing her college studies, Carolina made a bold decision: She would leave the United States for the Dominican Republic to reconnect with her heritage.

When Carolina arrived in Santo Domingo, she was hit with culture shock. Though she had grown up immersed in Dominican traditions, she was still American. More than ever, Carolina felt she did not completely belong to either culture. She also quickly became disheartened by the everyday negative stereotypes perpetuated against Afro-Latinas—she hated that Black hair was called *pelo malo* (bad hair) when it was anything but. Carolina craved systemic change—and personal change.

> **So, she made another bold decision:
> She cut her hair short and began experimenting
> with natural methods of caring for her curls.**

Letting her hair go natural was not an easy move for Carolina. Her mother was so concerned with what people would think that she threatened to relax Carolina's hair while she was sleeping. Her brother told her that her hair was "nappy" and that she didn't look pretty anymore. But Carolina was determined to help her family change their mindset, partly for the sake of younger generations. Why should her niece grow up being told to reject her natural hair just because a white-dominated culture claimed that only European features were beautiful?

Though it took her some time to figure out what worked, Carolina's natural hair was stunning. People would stop her in the streets just to ask how they could get *their* hair to look like hers! Carolina decided to share her newfound knowledge and experience by starting a blog, *Miss Rizos*, which quickly grew in popularity—first in Latin America and then around the world! Carolina used her expanding platform to explore issues of race and colorism in the Dominican Republic, empowering Afro-Latinas to celebrate their Blackness through the medium of hair. She wanted women like her to see that they were *already* beautiful and that they didn't need to conform to white culture.

Carolina became a powerful voice within the evolving natural hair movement. The popularity of her blog and social media presence inspired her to make yet another bold decision. In 2014, she opened the Miss Rizos Salon—the first natural hair salon in Santo Domingo!

> **It was a place where women with curly hair
> were supported, nourished, and educated.**

Miss Rizos was so popular that Dominican expatriates would fly home just to receive a haircut from Carolina! But it wasn't only the cut that drew them home: It felt good to visit a place where they were celebrated, just as they were.

By returning to her natural hair, Carolina reclaimed a part of herself and inspired others to follow in her footsteps. Her blog and her salon not only provide safe spaces for Afro-Latinas to celebrate themselves but also have helped the natural hair movement spread even farther throughout Latin America. In a culture where Black women are often discriminated against because of the texture of their hair, Carolina's voice reverberates—a joyful call to awaken a shared sense of beauty and identity, as well as a potent reminder of the power of self-love.

WIT LÓPEZ

{ Artist
1986–
Heritage: Puerto Rican }

WIT LÓPEZ learned early on to celebrate the body they lived in, even when acceptance by others was difficult to come by. As a child, Wit was diagnosed with attention deficit hyperactivity disorder (ADHD), autism spectrum disorder, and Osgood-Schlatter disease. The latter left them with bone chips in their knees that made certain kinds of movement painful. But Wit refused to let this challenge stop them from finding ways to do what they loved most.

Wit's parents were talented visual artists who passed on their skills to their two children, teaching them collage, fiber art, painting, and photography. Wit sold their first pair of earrings when they were only four years old!

> But it was their older sister, Oriana, whom they most aspired to be like.

Oriana's artwork was so striking that she was offered a scholarship to study ceramics at the Pratt Institute in Brooklyn. This was so impressive that Wit wanted to study there, too! They worked hard to refine their skills and were eventually awarded a scholarship for drawing classes at Pratt, just like Oriana.

Though Wit enjoyed art, there was nothing in the world they loved more than performing. They first took the stage when they were just two years old, and they frequently performed at church services. At school, Wit joined the choir and began taking music and dance lessons. They also learned to play both flute and piano, and they developed a strong mezzo-soprano voice. But performing eventually took a toll on Wit's body. Dance and stage work were painful!

> Still, Wit would not give up doing what they loved. It was time to find *new* forms of expression.

After several years of study in art history and administration, Wit put the skills garnered throughout their childhood to use as a means of exploring and expressing their identity. They posed in photographs that reflected gender fluidity and reimagined traditional beauty standards, examining hairiness, accessibility, Blackness, and Latinidad through different poses and costumes. Wit received grant money from the Independence Foundation and used it to put together an exhibition on seating, exploring the daily challenges faced by people with mobility issues. And on one occasion, they expressed their gender nonconformity by performing a bomba—an Afro-Boricuan dance and musical tradition—barefoot, instead of in traditionally "male" or "female" shoes.

Though Wit's art often explores painful experiences, it does so with levity and humor, enabling those who have lived through trauma to relate while still spotlighting systemic issues. They are tireless in their advocacy for inclusivity, encouraging audiences to interact with their art and ensuring that all of their exhibitions are accessible.

> By refusing to conform to societal preconceptions of what gender, ability, and beauty should look like, Wit creates work that people around the world can see themselves in.

Wit's art challenges audiences to examine their identities, powerfully subverting the idea that any of us are "less than" because of who we are.

JILLIAN MERCADO

Model and Activist
1987–
Heritage: Dominican

Before she became a model, JILLIAN MERCADO grew up on the *other* side of fashion, surrounded by the textures of fabrics and the painstaking work that went into making an article of clothing. Her mother was a seamstress in a factory, and her father sold shoes in Manhattan. Jillian loved to sit beside her mother as she sewed, watching her work and asking her lots of questions.

She was fascinated by the textures, colors, and designs of every piece of fabric.

Both parents helped her appreciate the finer details of clothing, contributing to her strong fashion sense—a sense that was also influenced by the colorful apparel of Jillian's Dominican culture, the women around her always polished and meticulously attired. She was inspired by the models she saw on TV, on billboards, and in magazines, dreaming that someday she might pose beside them on the runway.

But there was a problem with this dream: Jillian had never seen even one disabled model on a billboard or in the pages of a magazine. However deserving she believed herself to be, modeling seemed impossible. As a child, Jillian had been diagnosed with a disorder called *muscular dystrophy*, which caused a weakening of her muscles and made it difficult to walk. She used a motorized wheelchair to get around—a challenge in busy New York City! She had to get up earlier than others to deal with broken subway elevators and taxis that refused to pick her up. But the first time Jillian visited Times Square, she looked up at the billboards in awe. The people in those pictures were quite literally larger than life! Jillian was mesmerized.

> **Was there a place for people who used wheelchairs, like her, in those powerful images?**

Maybe not yet. But Jillian believed *she* could do something to change that.

Intent on transforming the fashion industry from within, Jillian decided to enroll at the Fashion Institute of Technology, where she studied marketing. To make the industry more equitable, Jillian would become a fashion editor! That way, she could hire disabled models and reach readers of *all* abilities. After graduating, Jillian learned the ins and outs of the fashion industry working as an intern at *Allure* magazine. Then, in 2013, she got word of an open casting call for Diesel, a well-known clothing company. Though Jillian had no intention of becoming a model, her friends encouraged her to apply.

> **When asked why she wanted to participate in the campaign, she said she wanted to change the world.**

In the end, Jillian was one of only twenty-three people from around the globe selected by Diesel. She—a disabled model—was going to be featured in the very magazines she'd read growing up!

Just two years later, Jillian was signed by an elite modeling agency called the International Management Group (IMG). She was cast in photoshoots for large department stores, such as Nordstrom and Target, and for celebrity merchants like Beyoncé.

> **But nothing compared to the moment when Jillian looked up and saw her own face on a billboard in Times Square—as a featured model in beauty brand Olay's "Face Anything" campaign.**

The fashion industry was changing, little by little, and Jillian was helping bring about that change.

Jillian used her new platform to push the industry toward broader representation of all races and abilities. Including people with disabilities in major ad campaigns was an important step, but she knew there was still more work to do. In 2018, Jillian joined Mama Cax and Chelsea Werner as the first disabled models to star on the cover of *Teen Vogue* magazine. The publication sought to center the voices of people with disabilities and remedy its exclusion of disabled models going forward. Two years later, she made her debut at New York Fashion Week, where she worked the runway in her wheelchair, decked out in a stunning gold jumpsuit and matching headpiece.

> **Jillian dedicated the moment to anyone with disabilities who, like her, had previously felt invisible in the fashion world—and, in doing so, sent a powerful message regarding societal perceptions of beauty.**

Jillian has asserted that it isn't enough for the fashion industry to include models with disabilities from time to time—their presence has to be *normalized*. She helps show the world that *everyone* deserves to have their own beauty represented.

ELIZABETH ACEVEDO

{ **Writer and Poet**
1988–
Heritage: Dominican }

ELIZABETH ACEVEDO learned early on that stories hold power. Her childhood was rich with family stories of life back in the Dominican Republic, as well as with the lyricism of Dominican bolero and New York City hip-hop. Elizabeth's parents were immigrants who spoke very little English, which meant she was left with the weighty responsibility of translating for the family. When she was twelve, she began writing songs and rapping about social issues she had learned about in school. Through verse, she told her *own* stories to anyone who would listen.

It wasn't until high school, when she joined a club called the Live Poets Society, that Elizabeth was first introduced to slam poetry. She had dreamed of becoming a rapper, but she decided to give poetry a try—and soon she was performing at open mics, where her natural abilities blossomed. Elizabeth *loved* performing slam.

> She found a freedom in spitting rhyme that she didn't always find in writing poetry.

But Elizabeth's journey was only beginning—there was still so much to learn!

After high school, Elizabeth enrolled in George Washington University and earned her bachelor's degree in performing arts. She felt lucky to have had the help of supportive teachers, so when her studies were completed, Elizabeth decided she wanted to be that support for others. She taught 150 students with Teach for America, most of whom were Latine but had *never* had an Afro-Latine teacher before. She tried to bring her love of the written word into the classroom, but her students were often uninspired by books, which frequently lacked relevance to their own lives.

> Elizabeth was frustrated by the lack of diverse representation in literature. She wanted things to change, and she saw no reason why *she* couldn't be the one to change them.

Determined to alter the literary canon to reflect the diversity of its readers, Elizabeth moved to Maryland and earned a master's degree in creative writing. She published her first collection of poetry in 2016, just two years after she was named a National Slam Champion. The book, *Beastgirl & Other Origin Myths*, was a collection of folk-infused poetry that centered on Elizabeth's cultural experience as a first-generation Dominican immigrant. Two years later, she published a novel in verse about a teenage Dominican American poet struggling to find her voice against the backdrop of Catholic immigrant culture.

> *The Poet X* was a literary triumph, receiving a Pura Belpré Award, a National Book Award for Young People's Literature, and many other accolades.

Though Elizabeth was pleased with her book's success, it wasn't the critical recognition that thrilled her, but rather the knowledge that she had created something readers could truly relate to.

Elizabeth's voice—both onstage and on the page—has impacted the literary world, empowering readers whose stories have gone untold for far too long.

> By centering underrepresented voices, she has created stories that are accessible to both children and adults—to *anyone* who can finally see themselves represented in her books.

Elizabeth's work has changed the literary canon for the better, demonstrating to dazzling effect the results of marginalized people shaping—and sharing—their own stories as *they* see fit.

DIOR VARGAS

{ Activist
1987–
Heritage: Ecuadorian }

When she was growing up, **DIOR VARGAS** felt alone in her sadness. Her family didn't talk about things like depression, and the TV commercials and magazines she saw that *did* talk about mental health featured only white people who looked nothing like Dior or her family.

Often, it was hard for Dior to feel safe.

Her parents sometimes had violent fights, and when she was seven years old, they divorced. At school, another girl made fun of her constantly. There was no one she felt she could talk to. There were times when she felt that happiness was, and always would be, impossible.

Things became especially challenging for Dior when she moved away for college. She had never been away from her family, and she still didn't fit in at school. Her college's community was mostly white, and when she didn't get along with her roommate, she was forced to move into a room by herself. Dior felt more alone than ever.

When she returned home for the summer, Dior thought that maybe now she would finally start to feel happy. But ignoring her sadness didn't make it go away. After intense fights with her mother and sister and an attempt to take her own life, Dior was admitted to the hospital and moved to a psychiatric ward. There she felt again like there was no one to talk to.

How could people who didn't look like her ever understand how she felt or where she came from?

It was hard, but Dior slowly recovered. With therapy and medication, she began to explore new ways of processing and coping with her feelings. She learned about the science of anxiety and depression, and she began talking openly with her family about the trauma of her childhood. It took a lot of courage, but Dior finally felt like she was taking charge of her mental health. With commitment and self-compassion, she was recovering.

In 2014, Dior started thinking about ways she could use her experience to help her community. She believed it was wrong for so many people's struggles with mental health to go unaddressed. There were so many roadblocks keeping people of color from getting help when they needed it—family biases, societal stigmas, and financial hardship among them.

Dior launched a photo campaign to bring awareness to these glaring issues, providing a source of support and encouragement for other people of color to share their mental health struggles.

The campaign got off to a slow start, in part due to the fear of stigma, so Dior decided to be brave and lead the way, sharing her picture and mental health story with the world first. Gradually, more and more people began to participate, sending in photographs and stories of their own. Dior was encouraged, but it was not enough. She saw a desperate need for more culturally aware health care workers who would be better able to address the mental health needs of Latine communities.

To help create such change, Dior went back to school to study public health. She received her master's degree from New York University while at the same time continuing her campaign. She was asked to speak publicly all over the country, sharing the story of her mental health journey and urging others to seek help when they needed it.

Though it was hard to speak so openly about her past traumas, Dior believed her voice was needed.

If *she* could take charge of her mental well-being, then so could others in her community. More than anything, she hoped to empower other Latine people to prioritize self-care.

In 2015, Dior was named a Champion of Change for Disability Advocacy Across Generations by Barack Obama's White House. Her work has provided an opportunity for communities of color to begin talking openly about mental health and to see that having anxiety, depression, or any other mental illness is *nothing* to be ashamed of.

Dior has worked hard to challenge the stigmas that kept so many silent, while also pushing for systemic change within the health care system.

By challenging the notion that mental illness is strictly a "white" concern, and by openly identifying as a queer and feminist activist, she has opened the door for people of all backgrounds to find their way to healing.

ALEXANDRIA OCASIO-CORTEZ

{ Activist and Politician
1989–
Heritage: Puerto Rican }

ALEXANDRIA OCASIO-CORTEZ knew the struggles of working-class families from firsthand experience. Though she was born in the Bronx, her family moved to the upscale suburb of Yorktown Heights was she was five years old, hoping to enroll Alexandria and her brother in the neighborhood's affluent public school.

> She spent much of her childhood visiting her friends and family in the Bronx, becoming aware of the vast income disparities between the two neighborhoods as she traveled between them.

The houses, infrastructure, and schools in Yorktown Heights benefited from the privilege of its populace, while the working-class people of the Bronx were left to do the best they could with what they had. These inequalities hit close to home, especially after Alexandria's father died and her house was put at risk of foreclosure.

Determined to make the most of the education her parents had sacrificed to give her, Alexandria studied hard and was accepted to Boston University, where she earned degrees in economics and international relations and interned with Senator Ted Kennedy.

> Her internship gave her an intimate look at the struggles of immigrants who had been separated from their families, and, soon after it ended, she decided to return to the Bronx to work on educational programs that supported undocumented youth.

Like many of her generation, Alexandria spent her twenties living paycheck to paycheck. She worked shifts as a waitress and bartender to help her family get by.

This period of Alexandria's life was marked by the Great Recession, a time when the disparity between high- and low-income earners was strikingly apparent. She watched as the federal government bailed out big banks, while families like her own were left to struggle. She was angry that the people who were supposed to represent her in the government valued the wealth of corporations more than the environment or equal access to health care. Fed up with waiting for change, Alexandria began campaigning for candidates she felt were dedicated to making a difference. In 2016, she volunteered for Bernie Sanders, a presidential candidate who shared her belief in fighting for the working classes. He lost his bid for the presidency, but Alexandria was energized. She decided to run for Congress as a representative of New York's 14th district, challenging a ten-term Democratic incumbent. Alexandria ran a grassroots campaign, relying on individual donations and refusing corporate money. In 2018, she won the election with 80 percent of the vote, becoming the youngest woman ever elected to Congress!

AOC, as she was now widely known, became a political celebrity overnight. She fought for programs like Medicare for All, moved to increase corporate taxes and reduce military spending, and led the push for a Green New Deal that would help fight climate change. She held regular livestreams where she discussed policy with her social media followers while making dinner or assembling furniture.

> She was young, charismatic, and unafraid of speaking her mind.

Not everyone approved of Alexandria's ambitious policy proposals and outspoken approach. Sometimes, she was targeted in ways that stank of sexism and prejudice, such as in 2020, when she was verbally accosted by a congressman. But Alexandria had grown a thick skin from her years of working in the service industry. She would not let herself, or the people around her, be dragged down or dehumanized, and she responded with a speech that decried verbal abuse and harassment directed toward women.

Throughout her tenure in Congress, Alexandria has fought for a better world, introducing legislation to protect the environment while also championing workers' rights. She has called for an end to immigrant detention, supported health care for all citizens, advocated for free college tuition, and pushed for renewable energy.

> Her views and policies are shaped by her belief that *everyone* deserves to be happy, regardless of where they come from, what they look like, or how much money they make.

Even when the opposition is fierce, Alexandria continues to fight so *all* people have a chance at the best possible life.

YALITZA APARICIO

{ Actor and Activist
1993–
Heritage: Mexican }

YALITZA APARICIO was born in Tlaxiaco, Mexico. Like the city itself, her family was a blend of Mixtec and Triqui people—two groups indigenous to the western state of Oaxaca, where Tlaxiaco is located.

Yalitza grew up understanding firsthand the daily hardships of Indigenous peoples in Mexico.

When she first started looking for work, she faced prejudice because of the color of her skin. Yalitza was determined to find a job where she could make a difference in her community, so she went to college and earned a degree in teaching.

Yalitza was excited to enter the classroom, but her plans changed unexpectedly when she accompanied her sister to a casting call. When they got there, her sister had a sudden change of heart and begged a reluctant Yalitza to audition in her place. The director was taken with her right away. He offered her the role, but she hesitated to accept. What about her plans to become a teacher? After thinking it through, she eventually agreed to take the part.

With no previous acting experience, Yalitza was cast in the starring role of a feature film.

The movie, *Roma*, was released to critical acclaim in 2018. Based on true events, it told the story of a young Indigenous woman working for an upper-class family, highlighting race and class disparities in Mexico. To develop her character, Yalitza drew on the struggles she had witnessed her mother face in day-to-day life as a domestic worker.

Her emotive performance moved audiences to tears and sparked a national conversation about the treatment of Indigenous peoples in Mexico.

She was nominated for an Academy Award for Best Actress in a Leading Role, making headlines as the first Indigenous American woman ever nominated in her category.

Her newfound fame led Yalitza to be featured on the covers of several prominent magazines, including *Vogue Mexico*. Her appearance, and the interviews she gave, broadened the public's perception of what it meant to be "beautiful," subverting harmful ideals that confined beauty to light skin and a tall, slender build. Yalitza felt the weight of her newfound responsibility to represent her community accurately—but she also realized that she was now in a position to spark real change for Indigenous communities, and she started using every opportunity to do so.

Yalitza's performance and activism led to notable changes within Mexico.

Just a year after *Roma*'s release, the government passed a law that provided domestic workers with protections they'd never had before, such as labor rights, a minimum wage, and retirement benefits. Yalitza also began pushing for the inclusion of Indigenous languages in education, hoping to both preserve those languages and keep Indigenous students from falling behind their Spanish-speaking peers. She supported the Mexican Commission for the Defense and Promotion of Human Rights and, in 2019, was named a United Nations Educational, Scientific and Cultural Organization (UNESCO) Goodwill Ambassador for Indigenous Peoples. With every interview and appearance, Yalitza works to give visibility to and elevate the voice of her community, teaching audiences around the world that speaking openly about prejudice is a necessary first step toward change.

INDYA MOORE

Actor, Model, and Activist
1995–
Heritage: Dominican, Haitian, Puerto Rican

INDYA MOORE grew up craving the freedom to be who they are. They were born in the Bronx to parents who didn't understand or accept that Indya was nonbinary—someone who was neither a girl nor a boy and did not conform to traditional gender norms.

> At school, they were bullied relentlessly. And at home, they were often punished just for being themself.

Tensions eventually got so bad that Indya entered foster care, and they dropped out of high school when they couldn't bear the bullying any longer. While in foster care, Indya met a transgender woman who let them try hormones to change their body—and for the first time, Indya's outside reflected who they were inside.

Indya liked the way they looked and started posting pictures on social media. They felt validated by the flood of positive comments they received and slowly began building a following. While they continued to suffer violence and abuse because of their identity—especially when their foster mom refused to continue giving them hormones—Indya felt that they had finally found a safer space on the internet. Their online community was growing every day. People all over the world thought Indya was beautiful.

> Their fans loved them for being openly transgender, for speaking out for the LGBTQ+ community, and for serving as a role model for others who struggled with anxiety and depression.

Indya's rapidly growing online presence led to runway modeling and photo shoots for big brands such as Dior and Gucci. Eventually, Indya was cast in *Pose*, a TV show about the ballroom culture of gender-nonconforming people during the 1980s. *Pose* boasted the largest cast of transgender actors for a scripted series in history. It was lauded by fans and critics alike, earning a Golden Globe nomination in its very first season.

Indya, fresh from foster care, was grateful for the life-changing opportunity. But some days on the set were challenging, forcing them to painfully relive past traumas. Many of the characters in *Pose* faced rejection and homelessness that mirrored Indya's own experiences. There were times when pushing through a scene would leave them and their castmates drained and on the verge of tears. But Indya would not give up on their dreams or themself. They weren't alone anymore, and their work was deeply meaningful to so many others.

Indya pushed forward, using their platform to advocate for the trans community and speaking openly about the systemic injustices that disproportionately affected people of color.

> They worked hard to bring visibility to the unique struggles of gender-nonconforming people and even helped raise money for the most marginalized members of the trans community.

In 2020, as the COVID-19 pandemic brought the world to its knees, Indya launched a Cash App campaign that raised thousands of dollars for some of the people who were hit hardest: Black transgender women. Indya's advocacy, presence on the runway, and vibrant onscreen performances have brought hope and inspiration to those who, like them, seek acceptance and deserve a life of dignity and celebration.

Despite the mistreatment Indya has received for being who they are, they have refused to give in to intolerance and hate and have fought hard for a sense of freedom. By speaking openly about their struggles, they have built their own community, always using their platform to lift the voices of transgender people everywhere.

JAMIE MARGOLIN

**Climate Justice Activist
2001–
Heritage: Colombian**

JAMIE MARGOLIN could not remember a time when she wasn't aware of climate change. Like most of her generation, she grew up unsettled about the future of our planet. All around her were signs that humanity was headed for an insurmountable ecological disaster, with extreme weather events like hurricanes and wildfires becoming more frequent with each passing year.

> Somebody *had* to do something to reverse the devastation around the world.

But the adults in charge of governments and corporations didn't seem to understand how very real the impending crisis was!

When Jamie was in second grade, she became so worried about climate change that she handed out "Save the Earth" buttons. She recycled, like they taught her at school, but her efforts did not feel big enough to create real change.

> Jamie felt frustrated by the relative inaction of the US government at every level, so she figured it was up to kids like her to ensure the planet's future.

Motivated to fight for substantive change, she began volunteering as an intern for Hillary Clinton's presidential campaign. At fourteen, Jamie was the youngest volunteer in the office—and the only one who was bilingual. As such, she was often pulled into meetings to provide Spanish translations. By observing how a high-level campaign was run, she learned quickly how to organize and take efficient civil action.

Jamie enjoyed volunteering, but she continued to feel that her efforts were not enough. In a push to do more, she began lobbying for environmental regulation at the city and state levels. She gave speeches within her community. She attended and organized climate-related events. But after a year of organizing, a sense of urgency still pulled at her. Everywhere she looked, marginalized communities were being hit especially hard by the climate emergency. In Puerto Rico, people's lives were upended by the devastation caused by Hurricane Maria. The air in her hometown of Seattle had grown dangerously polluted by wildfires in Canada's neighboring counties. As a queer person of color, Jamie took the situation personally, certain that the growing crisis would continue to disproportionately affect already struggling communities.

Jamie realized that now was the time to take real, decisive action.

> The adults of the world would have to be forced to address climate change.

She founded an organization called Zero Hour and planned a youth climate march in Washington, DC, using social media to encourage other kids to join her. Her efforts were successful, and the first march took place in July 2018. The following year, Jamie testified alongside Swedish youth activist Greta Thunberg in front of Congress, ahead of the United Nations Climate Action Summit in New York. Together, they pushed lawmakers to recognize the danger of continued complacency and urged them to take decisive action—to divest from fossil fuels, invest in renewable energies, undertake reforestation efforts, and lower carbon emissions. By bringing their concerns to the media and the courts, Jamie and her fellow youth activists inspired millions around the globe to pressure legislators for immediate and substantive change.

In 2020, while still a senior in high school, Jamie published her first book. *Youth to Power* is a guide to activism inspired by her own experiences as an organizer. Though it has sometimes been overwhelming to juggle growing up with the daily demands of her role as an activist, Jamie feels she has no choice.

> She *has* to fight to reclaim her generation's future.

She dreams of a day when kids like her will be able to live free of fear—a day when the institutions that have caused so much planetary suffering will be relegated to the realm of distant history.

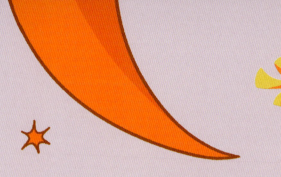

JHARREL JEROME

Actor
1997–
Heritage: Dominican

Growing up in the Bronx, **JHARREL JEROME** knew the story of the Central Park Five—five Black boys from Harlem who, in 1989, were unjustly prosecuted for a crime they did not commit. The story left an impression on Jharrel and his friends that they would never forget.

> People often judged or profiled them for being Black, but Jharrel was proud of who he was and of his community.

He loved the musical culture of the Bronx, where freestyle was poetry. He learned to rap off the top of his head when he was a young kid. But there were also limitations to living in the Bronx that Jharrel was keen to be free of. When he was thirteen, he decided to broaden his experiences and attend a school with specialty programs. His mother—considering Jharrel's penchant for drama—suggested he try acting. And even though he had never had a day of formal training, he decided to give it a shot.

Jharrel's mother bought the book *Monologues for Teens*, and they began rehearsing together. He auditioned for every performing arts school in the city—and was accepted to all of them!

> Jharrel chose to enroll at LaGuardia High School, famed for its celebrity alumni, and soon discovered he had both a passion and a natural talent for acting.

He was cast in school productions, where his innate charisma shone, and performed in front of the agents and managers who regularly scouted new talent at the school. During one such production, a manager fell in love with Jharrel's performance and offered to represent him. Jharrel was over the moon! He enthusiastically accepted.

Jharrel was the very first in his family to graduate from high school. After graduation, he enrolled at Ithaca College and continued to study acting. During his studies, Jharrel was cast in *Moonlight*, a film about a Black youth's struggles with his sexual identity amid abuse.

> The film was a critical success, winning an Academy Award for Best Picture and turning Jharrel into an overnight celebrity for his provocative performance.

Just a few years later, Jharrel was cast in *When They See Us*, a limited series about the Central Park Five. The harrowing story that Jharrel had heard as a boy was finally being retold from the perspective of the boys who had been so unjustly accused.

Jharrel's portrayal of Korey Wise was powerful, raw, and emotive, earning him an Emmy Award in the category of Best Lead Actor. The win was historic.

> Jharrel was the first Afro-Latine actor, *and* the first Dominican actor, to ever win an Emmy in this category!

But even more important, the success of the show sparked a national conversation. People were finally talking about the injustice of the Central Park Five case and pushing for reform to a justice system fraught with discrimination. Jharrel dedicated his Emmy to the Exonerated Five, who were present in the audience and watched tearfully as he accepted his award. He was only twenty-one—the youngest actor in history to win in this category. With award-winning performances behind him and a brilliant career ahead, Jharrel has shown the world just how much a kid from the Bronx can do.

SOPHIE CRUZ

Activist
2010–
Heritage: Mexican

When **SOPHIE CRUZ** was five years old, she had one wish: to visit her abuelo. Sophie lived in the United States, but her grandfather lived in Mexico, and she wanted to meet him. When her parents said no, Sophie learned that they were at risk for deportation if they ever left the country. Unlike Sophie and her sister, who had been born in the United States, Sophie's parents were undocumented. She was scared.

> What if they were deported someday? What would happen to Sophie and her sister if their family was separated?

She told her parents that there was only one thing to do. They would fight for the family's right to remain together.

After seeking the help of an immigration advocacy organization, Sophie was invited by the group to Washington, DC, for a chance to see the visiting pope. She sat on her father's shoulders to see over the crowd, but when Pope Francis's motorcade drove by, she asked him to put her down so she could get the pope's attention. Excited, Sophie ran toward his car—but she was stopped by security before she could get close. The pope, however, had seen Sophie running toward him, and he graciously waved her forward.

> She was lifted up to the pope's car, where she hugged him and gave him a letter in which she spoke of the struggles of immigrants like her parents.

She asked him to speak to Congress, and to the president, about their plight. Deeply moved by Sophie's letter, the pope spoke with Congress about immigration the very next day.

Shortly after the pope's speech, Sophie was invited to the White House to express her concerns in person to the president. A couple of years later, she was asked to speak before hundreds of thousands of people at the Women's March in Washington, DC.

> With her parents and sister beside her, Sophie addressed the audience in both English and Spanish, inciting the crowd to chant "Sí se puede!"—"Yes, it can be done!"—as a rallying cry for immigration reform.

She later attended the Supreme Court hearings on Deferred Action for Parents of Americans (DAPA), which would have granted parents of US citizens—like Sophie's—protection from deportation if it had passed. Unfortunately, the order was blocked, and the incoming president, Donald J. Trump, eventually rescinded it altogether. But Sophie's fighting spirit ignited hope in immigrants and activists across the country. Her touching words, honest spirit, and deep love for her family have resonated with citizens who, just like Sophie, only wish for their loved ones to be granted the freedoms they deserve. Her ongoing advocacy for immigrant rights has been a beacon of light in the dark, giving voice to millions of people fighting for an end to family separation.

Selected Bibliography

Celia Cruz

CeliaCruz.com. "Celia Cruz Biography." Accessed May 3, 2024. https://celiacruz.com/biography/.

Encyclopaedia Britannica. "Celia Cruz." Updated April 26, 2024. www.britannica.com/biography/Celia-Cruz.

Fernández, Stefanie. "Celia Cruz's 'Son Con Guaguancó' and the Bridge to Fame in Exile." NPR. February 13, 2018. www.npr.org/2018/02/13/584004511/celia-cruzs-son-con-guaguanc-and-the-bridge-to-fame-in-exile.

VOA. "Celia Cruz, 1925–2003: 'The Queen of Salsa.'" May 7, 2011. https://learningenglish.voanews.com/a/celia-cruz-1925-2003-the-queen-of-salsa-121440804/114425.html.

Waring, Charles. "Celia Cruz: Celebrating the Queen of Salsa." uDiscoverMusic. October 21, 2023. www.udiscovermusic.com/stories/celia-cruz-latin-singer-salsa/.

Matilde Hidalgo

Herbert, Tom. "Who Was Matilde Hidalgo de Procel? Today's Google Doodle Celebrates Trailblazing Activist Who Was First Woman to Vote in Latin America." *Standard*, November 21, 2019. www.standard.co.uk/lifestyle/london-life/matilde-hidalgo-de-procel-google-doodle-activist-a4292541.html.

Parfitt, Tom. "Matilde Hidalgo: Who Was the Trailblazing Doctor and Women's Rights Activist?" *Independent*, November 21, 2019. www.independent.co.uk/news/world/americas/matilde-hidalgo-de-procel-google-doodle-today-ecuador-doctor-death-who-a9211751.html.

Antônio Carlos Jobim

Encyclopedia.com. "Jobim, Antônio Carlos 'Tom' (1927–1994)." April 16, 2024. www.encyclopedia.com/humanities/encyclopedias-almanacs-transcripts-and-maps/jobim-antonio-carlos-tom-1927-1994.

Fresh Air. "Celebrating 30 Years of 'Fresh Air': Brazilian Composer Antônio Carlos Jobim." NPR. August 25, 2017. www.npr.org/2017/08/25/546070127/celebrating-30-years-of-fresh-air-brazilian-composer-ant-nio-carlos-jobim.

Gorlinski, Virginia. "Antônio Carlos Jobim." Encyclopaedia Britannica. Updated April 25, 2024. www.britannica.com/biography/Antonio-Carlos-Jobim.

Grimes, William. "António Carlos Jobim, Composer, Dies at 67." *New York Times*, December 9, 1994. www.nytimes.com/1994/12/09/obituaries/antonio-carlos-jobim-composer-dies-at-67.html.

Songwriters Hall of Fame. "Antonio Carlos Jobim: Father of Brazil's Bossa Nova." Accessed May 3, 2024. www.songhall.org/profile/Antonio_Carlos_Jobim.

Eva Perón (Evita)

Biography.com. "Eva Perón." Updated May 6, 2021. www.biography.com/political-figures/eva-peron.

Encyclopaedia Britannica. "Eva Perón." Updated April 1, 2024. www.britannica.com/biography/Eva-Peron.

Larson, Dolane J. *Evita's World: The Defining Years, 1919–1947*. North Charleston, SC: Create Space Independent Publishing Platform, 2016.

Sky History. "Evita." Accessed May 3, 2024. www.history.co.uk/biographies/evita.

Pura Belpré

American Library Association. "Pura Belpré Award." Accessed May 3, 2024. www.ala.org/alsc/awardsgrants/bookmedia/belpre.

Center for Puerto Rican Studies–Centro. "Pura Belpré: More than Storyteller." YouTube video, 95:51 min. March 28, 2014. www.youtube.com/watch?v=fYy0no0dZv4.

New York Public Library. "Pura Belpré: Library Storyteller." November 12, 2020. www.nypl.org/blog/2020/11/12/pura-belpre-library-storyteller.

Ulaby, Neda. "How NYC's First Puerto Rican Librarian Brought Spanish to the Shelves." NPR. September 8, 2016. www.npr.org/2016/09/08/492957864/how-nycs-first-puerto-rican-librarian-brought-spanish-to-the-shelves.

Lucila Godoy Alcagaya (Gabriela Mistral)

Alexander, Kerri Lee. "Gabriela Mistral." National Women's History Museum. 2019. www.womenshistory.org/education-resources/biographies/gabriela-mistral.

Encyclopaedia Britannica. "Gabriela Mistral." Updated April 3, 2024. www.britannica.com/biography/Gabriela-Mistral.

Gabriela Mistral Foundation. "Gabriela Mistral." Accessed May 3, 2024. https://mistralnobel45.wixsite.com/gmf2007/nota-autobiografica.

Library of Congress. "Gabriela Mistral." Accessed May 3, 2024. www.loc.gov/item/n50033817/gabriela-mistral-chile-1889-1957/.

Nobel Prize, The. "Gabriela Mistral Facts." Accessed May 3, 2024. www.nobelprize.org/prizes/literature/1945/mistral/facts/.

José Castellanos Contreras

BESE. "The Secret Mission of Castellanos and Mandl | Hidden Figuras." YouTube video, 3:57 min. October 1, 2018. www.youtube.com/watch?v=oeBnr4RCQdA.

Clarfield, Geoffrey. "Righteous among the Nations: The Rescued Tribe of Colonel Jose Arturo Castellanos Contreras." *Quillette*, October 11, 2018. https://quillette.com/2018/10/11/righteous-among-the-nations-the-rescued-tribe-of-colonel-jose-arturo-castellanos-contreras/.

International Fellowship of Christians and Jews. "Saving 40,000 'Salvadorans' from the Holocaust." July 31, 2023. www.ifcj.org/news/stand-for-israel-blog/saving-40000-salvadorans-from-the-holocaust.

Russell, Shahan. "José Arturo Castellanos Contreras: The Latino Schindler." War History Online. March 22, 2017. www.warhistoryonline.com/history/jose-arturo-castellanos-contreras-latino-schindler.html.

World Jewish Congress. "Germany Pays Tribute to Salvadoran Savior of Tens of Thousands of Jews." May 12, 2016. www.worldjewishcongress.org/en/news/german-foreign-office-pays-tribute-to-salvadoran-savior-of-tens-of-thousands-of-jews-5-4-2016.

Wifredo Lam

Encyclopaedia Britannica. "Wifredo Lam." Updated April 30, 2024. www.britannica.com/biography/Wifredo-Lam.

Guggenheim. "Wifredo Lam." Accessed May 3, 2024. www.guggenheim.org/artwork/artist/wifredo-lam.

Museum of Modern Art. "Wifredo Lam." Accessed May 3, 2024. www.moma.org/artists/3349#main.

Paudrat, Jean-Louis. "Wifredo Lam: Biography." WifredoLam.net. Accessed May 3, 2024. www.wifredolam.net/en/biography.html.

Tate. "Who Is Wifredo Lam?" Accessed May 3, 2024. www.tate.org.uk/whats-on/tate-modern/wifredo-lam/who-is.

Amalia Hernández

El Periódico. "Amalia Hernández: ¿Quién fue y cómo revolucionó el baile en México?" September 19, 2017. www.elperiodico.com/es/extra/20170919/amalia-hernandez-6295139.

Mariachi Tradicional Femenil Flores de México. "Documentary on the Ballet Folklórico de México de Amalia Hernández." YouTube video, 51:56 min. April 17, 2018. www.youtube.com/watch?v=hV6giUZakQ1.

Smith, James F. "Amalia Hernandez; Creator of Mexico's Ballet Folklorico." *Los Angeles Times*, November 5, 2000. www.latimes.com/archives/la-xpm-2000-nov-05-me-47382-story.html.

Frida Kahlo

Biography.com. "Frida Kahlo." Updated November 19, 2021. www.biography.com/artists/frida-kahlo.

FridaKahlo.org. "Frida Kahlo Biography." Accessed May 3, 2024. www.fridakahlo.org/frida-kahlo-biography.jsp.

Museum of Modern Art. "Frida Kahlo." Accessed May 3, 2024. www.moma.org/artists/2963.

Tuchman, Phyllis. "Frida Kahlo." *Smithsonian Magazine*, November 2002. www.smithsonianmag.com/arts-culture/frida-kahlo-70745811/.

Zelazko, Alicja. "Frida Kahlo." Encyclopaedia Britannica. Updated March 21, 2024. www.britannica.com/biography/Frida-Kahlo.

Violeta Parra

Arcos, Betto. "In 'Violeta Went to Heaven,' a Folk Icon's Tempestuous Life." NPR. July 13, 2013. www.npr.org/2013/07/13/201227290/in-violeta-went-to-heaven-a-folk-icons-tempestuous-life.

Blau, Jnan Ananda. "Violeta Parra." Encyclopaedia Britannica. Updated February 1, 2024. www.britannica.com/biography/Violeta-Parra.

Cicchetto, Susana. "Violeta Parra, Chilean Singer and Composer (1917–1967)." LatinoLife. Accessed May 3, 2024. www.latinolife.co.uk/articles/violeta-parra-chilean-singer-and-composer-1917-1967.

Encyclopedia.com. "Parra, Violeta (1917–1967)." April 15, 2024. www.encyclopedia.com/humanities/encyclopedias-almanacs-transcripts-and-maps/parra-violeta-1917-1967.

Salient Women. "Biography of Violeta Parra, Chilean Singer." Accessed May 3, 2024. www.salientwomen.com/2020/05/22/biography-of-violeta-parra-chilean-singer-artist/.

Ildaura Murillo-Rohde

Broome, Marion E., and Elaine Sorensen Marshall. "Six Transformational 20th Century Nurse Leaders." Daily Nurse. May 14, 2020. https://dailynurse.com/?s=Ildaura+Murillo-Rohde.

Portillo, Carmen. "25 and Counting." Minority Nurse. March 30, 2013. https://minoritynurse.com/?s=Ildaura+Murillo-Rohde.

Weiner, Stacy. "Celebrating 10 Hispanic Pioneers in Medicine." Association of American Medical Colleges. September 17, 2020. www.aamc.org/news/celebrating-10-hispanic-pioneers-medicine/.

Tito Puente

Biography.com. "Tito Puente." Updated October 28, 2021. www.biography.com/musicians/tito-puente.

DeGraf, Galen P. "Situating *Salsa* through Tito Puente's Life and Music." Bachelor's honors thesis, Wesleyan University, 2009. https://digitalcollections.wesleyan.edu/_flysystem/fedora/2023-03/22392-Original%20File.pdf.

Encyclopaedia Britannica. "Tito Puente." Updated April 26, 2024. www.britannica.com/biography/Tito-Puente.

Smithsonian. "Tito Puente." Accessed May 3, 2024. www.si.edu/spotlight/latin-music-legends-stamps/tito-puente.

Wadler, Joyce. "Tito Puente, Famed Master of Latin Music, Is Dead at 77." *New York Times*, June 2, 2000. www.nytimes.com/2000/06/02/arts/tito-puente-famed-master-of-latin-music-is-dead-at-77.html.

Gabriel García Márquez

Anderson, Jon Lee. "The Power of García Márquez." *New Yorker*, September 27, 1999. www.newyorker.com/magazine/1999/09/27/the-power-of-garcia-marquez.

Kandell, Jonathan. "Gabriel García Márquez, Conjurer of Literary Magic, Dies at 87." *New York Times*, April 17, 2014. www.nytimes.com/2014/04/18/books/gabriel-garcia-marquez-literary-pioneer-dies-at-87.html.

Simons, Marlise. "The Best Years of His Life: An Interview with Gabriel García Márquez." *New York Times*, April 10, 1988. www.nytimes.com/1988/04/10/books/the-best-years-of-his-life-an-interview-with-gabriel-garcia-marquez.html.

César Milstein

American Association of Immunologists, The. "César Milstein, PhD." Accessed May 3, 2024. www.aai.org/About/History/Notable-Members/Nobel-Laureates/CesarMilstein.

Encyclopaedia Britannica. "César Milstein." Updated March 27, 2024. www.britannica.com/biography/Cesar-Milstein.

Rabbitts, Terence H. "César Milstein." *Cell Press* 105, no. 5 (May 31, 2002): 549–50. www.cell.com/fulltext/S0092-8674(02)00760-2.

Warmflash, David. "Revolutionizing Medicine with Monoclonal Antibodies: The Work of César Milstein." Visionlearning. 2015. www.visionlearning.com/en/library/scientists-and-research/58/revolutionzining-medicine-with-monoclonal-antibodies/220.

WhatIsBiotechnology. "Professor Cesar Milstein." Accessed May 3, 2024. www.whatisbiotechnology.org/index.php/people/summary/Milstein.

Dolores Huerta

Bratt, Peter, dir. *Dolores*. 2017; PBS Distribution.

Dolores Huerta Foundation for Community Organizing. "Dolores Huerta." Accessed May 3, 2024. https://doloreshuerta.org/dolores-huerta/.

Encyclopaedia Britannica. "Dolores Huerta." Updated April 23, 2024. www.britannica.com/biography/Dolores-Huerta.

Godoy, Maria. "Dolores Huerta: The Civil Rights Icon Who Showed Farmworkers 'Sí Se Puede.'" NPR. September 17, 2017. www.npr.org/sections/thesalt/2017/09/17/551490281/dolores-huerta-the-civil-rights-icon-who-showed-farmworkers-si-se-puede.

López, Carlos Andres. "Dolores Huerta: 'We Have to Keep on Marching.'" *New York Times*, October 7, 2020. www.nytimes.com/2020/10/07/opinion/international-world/dolores-huerta-activists-unions.html.

Jaime Escalante

Biography.com. "Jaime Escalante." Updated March 26, 2021. www.biography.com/scholars-educators/jaime-escalante.

Encyclopedia.com. "Escalante, Jaime: 1930–: Educator." Updated June 8, 2018. www.encyclopedia.com/people/social-sciences-and-law/political-science-biographies/jaime-escalante.

Futures Channel, The. "Jaime Escalante." Accessed May 3, 2024. https://thefutureschannel.com/educator-resources/jaime-escalante/.

Sanchez, Claudio. "Jaime Escalante's Legacy: Teaching Hope." NPR. March 31, 2010. www.npr.org/2010/03/31/125398451/jaime-escalantes-legacy-teaching-hope.

Woo, Elaine. "Jaime Escalante Dies at 79; Math Teacher Who Challenged East LA Students to 'Stand and Deliver.'" *Los Angeles Times*, April 25, 2013. www.latimes.com/local/obituaries/la-me-jaime-escalante31-2010mar31-story.html.

Rita Moreno

Alexander, Kerri Lee. "Rita Moreno." National Women's History Museum. 2019. www.womenshistory.org/education-resources/biographies/rita-moreno.

Gray, Tim. "How Rita Moreno Found Dignity and Strength with Her 'West Side Story' Role." *Variety*, December 11, 2020. https://variety.com/2020/film/news/rita-moreno-west-side-story-egot-1234843891/.

History.com. "This Day in History: Rita Moreno Becomes the First Hispanic Woman to Win an Oscar." Updated April 8, 2024. www.history.com/this-day-in-history/rita-moreno-first-hispanic-woman-to-win-oscar-west-side-story.

PBS NewsHour. "Rita Moreno Has the Time of Her Life on Stage and Screen." YouTube video, 4:36 min. December 10, 2015. www.youtube.com/watch?v=56oRHSM7vsM.

Tikkanen, Amy. "Rita Moreno." Encyclopaedia Britannica. Updated April 23, 2024. www.britannica.com/biography/Rita-Moreno.

Walter Mercado

Costantini, Cristina, and Kareem Tabsch, dirs. *Mucho Mucho Amor: The Legend of Walter Mercado*. 2020; Netflix.

Garcia, Sandra E. "Walter Mercado, Celebrity Astrologer for Millions of Latinos, Dies." *New York Times*, November 3, 2019. www.nytimes.com/2019/11/03/world/americas/walter-mercado-dead.html.

Leandra, Victoria. "Walter Mercado, Subject of a New Netflix Doc, Was the World's Most Famous Astrologer." Oprah Daily. July 9, 2020. www.oprahdaily.com/entertainment/a33265237/who-is-walter-mercado-mucho-mucho-amor/.

Schulman, Michael. "The Improbable Charisma of Walter Mercado." *New Yorker*, July 24, 2020. www.newyorker.com/culture/culture-desk/the-improbable-charisma-of-walter-mercado.

Wood, Douglas. "Popular Astrologer Walter Mercado Dies at 87." CNN. Updated November 3, 2019. www.cnn.com/2019/11/03/entertainment/walter-mercado-dies-trnd/index.html.

Roberto Clemente

Jamail, Milton. "Roberto Clemente." Encyclopaedia Britannica. Updated April 5, 2024. www.britannica.com/biography/Roberto-Clemente.

Klein, Christopher. "How Puerto Rican Baseball Icon Roberto Clemente Left a Legacy off the Field." History.com. Updated June 1, 2023. www.history.com/news/roberto-clemente-humanitarian-accomplishments-pittsburgh-pirates.

Mr. Nussbaum. "Roberto Clemente Biography." Accessed May 3, 2024. https://mrnussbaum.com/roberto-clemente-biography.

National Baseball Hall of Fame. "Roberto Clemente." Accessed May 3, 2024. https://baseballhall.org/hall-of-famers/clemente-roberto.

Roberto Clemente Foundation. "Roberto's Story." Accessed May 3, 2024. www.robertoclementefoundation.org/roberto-clemente-bio/.

Sylvia Mendez

Russian, Ale. "Sylvia Mendez and Her Parents Fought School Segregation Years before 'Brown v. Board.'" Biography.com. September 15, 2020. www.biography.com/activists/sylvia-mendez-school-segregation-fight.

Sylvia Mendez School PTA. "Who Is Sylvia Mendez?—Separate Is Never Equal." Accessed May 3, 2024. www.sylviamendezschool.org/who-is-sylvia-mendez.

Tonatiuh, Duncan. *Separate Is Never Equal: Sylvia Mendez and Her Family's Fight for Desegregation*. New York: Abrams, 2014.

Yoshiko Kandil, Caitlin. "Mendez vs. Segregation: 70 Years Later, Famed Case 'Isn't Just about Mexicans. It's about Everybody Coming Together.'" *Los Angeles Times*, April 17, 2016. www.latimes.com/socal/daily-pilot/tn-wknd-et-0417-sylvia-mendez-70-anniversary-20160417-story.html.

Florentina López de Jesús

Amigos de los Grandes Maestros del Arte Popular. "Florentina-Lopez-Jesus." Accessed May 3, 2024. https://amigosgrandesmaestros.org/florentina-lopez-jesus/.

Briscoe, Kienan. "Lynnwood Councilwoman Preserves the Legacy of Indigenous Artist at Paris-Sorbonne University." *Lynnwood Times*, July 20, 2023. https://lynnwoodtimes.com/2023/07/20/altamirano-crosby-lopez-de-jesus-2307/.

Feria Maestros del Arte. "Florentina López de Jesús (1939–2014), Xochistlahuaca, Guerrero." Accessed May 3, 2024. https://feriamaestros.com/pages/pprofileflorentinalopezdejesus.

Maria Bueno

Encyclopaedia Britannica. "Maria Bueno." February 19, 2024. www.britannica.com/biography/Maria-Ester-Audion-Bueno.

Encyclopedia.com. "Bueno, Maria (1939–)." April 16, 2024. www.encyclopedia.com/women/encyclopedias-almanacs-transcripts-and-maps/bueno-maria-1939.

Goldstein, Richard. "Maria Bueno, Brazilian Tennis Star Who Reigned over 1960s, Dies at 78." *New York Times*, June 9, 2018. www.nytimes.com/2018/06/09/obituaries/maria-bueno-dead-tennis.html.

International Tennis Hall of Fame. "Maria Bueno." Accessed May 3, 2024. www.tennisfame.com/hall-of-famers/inductees/maria-bueno.

MariaBueno.org. Home page. Accessed May 3, 2024. www.mariabueno.org/indextemp.php/.

Joan Baez

Browne, David. "Joan Baez's Fighting Side: The Life and Times of a Secret Badass." *Rolling Stone*, April 5, 2017. www.rollingstone.com/music/music-features/joan-baezs-fighting-side-the-life-and-times-of-a-secret-badass-129051/.

Encyclopaedia Britannica. "Joan Baez." Updated March 28, 2024. www.britannica.com/biography/Joan-Baez.

Encyclopedia.com. "Baez, Joan Chandos." April 15, 2024. www.encyclopedia.com/humanities/encyclopedias-almanacs-transcripts-and-maps/baez-joan-chandos.

Kellaway, Kate. "Joan Baez: 'Music Can Move People to Do Things.'" *Guardian*, February 24, 2019. www.theguardian.com/music/2019/feb/24/joan-baez-interview-whistle-down-the-wind-farewell-tour-folk-music-protest-songs.

Edson Arantes do Nascimento (Pelé)

Biography.com. "Pelé." Updated December 29, 2022. www.biography.com/athletes/pele.

Encyclopaedia Britannica. "Pelé." Updated April 11, 2024. www.britannica.com/biography/Pele-Brazilian-athlete.

Encyclopedia.com. "Pelé (1940–)." April 15, 2024. www.encyclopedia.com/humanities/encyclopedias-almanacs-transcripts-and-maps/pele-1940.

Gault, Matt. "Pelé: The Brazil Legend Yet to Be Toppled." *These Football Times*, August 22, 2017. https://thesefootballtimes.co/2017/08/22/pele-the-brazil-legend-yet-to-be-toppled/.

Talks. "Pelé: 'My Father and My Mother Closed the Machine.'" Accessed May 3, 2024. https://the-talks.com/interview/pele/.

Mario J. Molina

California Museum. "Mario J. Molina, PhD." Accessed May 3, 2024. https://californiamuseum.org/inductee/mario-j-molina-ph-d/.

Encyclopaedia Britannica. "Mario Molina." Updated March 15, 2024. www.britannica.com/biography/Mario-Molina.

Molina, Mario J. "Mario J. Molina Biographical." The Nobel Prize. November 2007. www.nobelprize.org/prizes/chemistry/1995/molina/biographical/.

Susana Baca

Aguirre, Carlos. "Susana Baca (1944–)." Black Past. September 29, 2011. www.blackpast.org/global-african-history/baca-susana-1944/.

Collyns, Dan. "Susana Baca: The Singer Who Became Peru's First Black Cabinet Minister." *Guardian*, October 28, 2011. www.theguardian.com/world/2011/oct/28/susana-baca-singer-peru-minister.

Dye, David. "Susana Baca: 'The Soul of Black Peru.'" NPR. June 14, 2006. www.npr.org/2006/06/14/5485803/susana-baca-the-soul-of-black-peru.

Encyclopedia.com. "Baca, Susana." April 15, 2024. www.encyclopedia.com/education/news-wires-white-papers-and-books/baca-susana.

Murray, Elisa. "Susana Baca." Roots World. Accessed May 3, 2024. www.rootsworld.com/rw/feature/baca.html.

Reverend Gérard Jean-Juste

Daniel, Nyamekye. "'Haitian Martin Luther King' Honored." *Miami Times*, April 10, 2019. www.miamitimesonline.com/lifestyles/haitian-martin-luther-king-honored/article_989322d4-5ba0-11e9-851d-5b4ce8fe3e1a.html.

Frogameni, Bill. "Haitian Activist Priest Jean-Juste Dies at 62." *National Catholic Reporter*, May 29, 2009. www.ncronline.org/news/people/haitian-activist-priest-jean-juste-dies-62.

Grimes, William. "The Rev. Gérard Jean-Juste, Champion of Haitian Rights in US, Dies at 62." *New York Times*, May 28, 2009. www.nytimes.com/2009/05/29/world/americas/29jean-juste.html.

Paulo Coelho

Biography.com. "Paulo Coelho." Updated November 6, 2019. www.biography.com/authors-writers/paulo-coelho.

Calvert, Michael T., Richard Pallardy, et al. "Paulo Coelho." Encyclopaedia Britannica. Updated April 30, 2024. www.britannica.com/biography/Paulo-Coelho.

Oprah. "Oprah Learns the Secret to Paulo Coelho's Timeless Wisdom." *O, The Oprah Magazine*, October 2014. www.oprah.com/inspiration/oprah-talks-to-the-alchemist-author-paulo-coelho/all.

Paulo Coelho and Christina Oiticica Foundation. "Paulo Coelho Biography." Accessed May 3, 2024. https://paulocoelhofoundation.com/paulo-coelho/biography/.

United Nations. "Paulo Coelho." Accessed May 3, 2024. www.un.org/en/messengers-peace/paulo-coelho.

Franklin Chang-Díaz

American Physical Society. "Franklin Chang-Diaz." Accessed May 3, 2024. www.aps.org/careers/physicists/profiles/changdiaz.cfm.

Encyclopaedia Britannica. "Franklin Chang-Díaz." Updated April 26, 2024. www.britannica.com/biography/Franklin-Chang-Diaz.

National Aeronautics and Space Administration. "Biographical Data: Franklin R. Chang-Díaz." September 2012. www.nasa.gov/wp-content/uploads/2016/01/chang-diaz_franklin_0.pdf.

NOVA ScienceNOW. "Franklin Chang-Díaz: Rocket Scientist." Video, 4:28 min. July 14, 2009. https://ny.pbslearningmedia.org/resource/nsn09.sci.engin.systems.diaz/franklin-chang-diaz-rocket-scientist/.

Sylvia Rivera

Devaney, Susan. "Who Was Sylvia Rivera? Marsha P. Johnson's Best Friend Was a Fellow Pioneer." *British Vogue*, June 13, 2020. www.vogue.co.uk/arts-and-lifestyle/article/who-was-sylvia-rivera.

Goodman, Elyssa. "Sylvia Rivera Changed Queer and Trans Activism Forever." *Them*, March 26, 2019. www.them.us/story/sylvia-rivera.

Klebine, Anna. "'Hell Hath No Fury Like a Drag Queen Scorned': Sylvia Rivera's Activism, Resistance, and Resilience." OutHistory. 2012. https://outhistory.org/exhibits/show/tgi-bios/sylvia-rivera.

Marcus, Eric. "'I Have to Go Off': Activist Sylvia Rivera on Choosing to Riot at Stonewall" (1989). *Guardian*, June 23, 2019. www.theguardian.com/us-news/2019/jun/23/i-have-to-go-off-activist-sylvia-rivera-on-choosing-to-riot-at-stonewall.

Reyes, Raul A. "A Forgotten Latina Trailblazer: LGBT Activist Sylvia Rivera." NBC News. October 6, 2015. www.nbcnews.com/news/latino/forgotten-latina-trailblazer-lgbt-activist-sylvia-rivera-n438586.

Sonia Sotomayor

Biography.com, and Colin McEvoy. "Sonia Sotomayor." Updated March 6, 2023. www.biography.com/legal-figures/sonia-sotomayor.

Daily Show, The. "Sonia Sotomayor—A Day in the Life of a Supreme Court Justice." YouTube video, 22:51 min. Aired September 16, 2019. www.youtube.com/watch?v=HcMhgKywE1c.

Oyez. "Sonia Sotomayor." Accessed May 3, 2024. www.oyez.org/justices/sonia_sotomayor.

White House: President Barack Obama, The. "Background on Judge Sonia Sotomayor." May 26, 2009. https://obamawhitehouse.archives.gov/the-press-office/background-judge-sonia-sotomayor.

Wolf, Richard. "'The People's Justice': After Decade on Supreme Court, Sonia Sotomayor Is Most Outspoken on Bench and Off." *USA Today*, August 8, 2019. www.usatoday.com/story/news/politics/2019/08/08/justice-sonia-sotomayor-supreme-court-liberal-hispanic-decade-bench/1882245001/.

María Elena Salinas

Allocca, Kevin. "So What Do You Do, Maria Elena Salinas, Univision Network News Anchor?" Mediabistro. Accessed May 3, 2024. www.mediabistro.com/interviews/so-what-do-you-do-maria-elena-salinas-univision-network-news-anchor/.

BillMoyers.com. "María Elena Salinas." Accessed May 3, 2024. https://billmoyers.com/guest/maria-elena-salinas/.

James, Meg. "CBS News Hires Univision Veteran Maria Elena Salinas." *Los Angeles Times*, July 22, 2019. www.latimes.com/entertainment-arts/business/story/2019-07-22/maria-elena-salinas-joins-cbs-news.

Matz, Jenni. "The Interviews: Maria Elena Salinas." *Emmy*, August 20, 2018. www.emmys.com/news/interviews-archive/interviews-maria-elena-salinas.

Salinas, María Elena. "María Elena Salinas Is American and Mexican Proud." AARP. August 1, 2018. www.aarp.org/politics-society/history/info-2018/maria-elena-salinas-hispanic-heritage-month.html.

Maricel Presilla

Giller, Megan. "Maricel Presilla, Culinary Historian and Chocolate Expert." Chocolate Noise. Accessed May 3, 2024. www.chocolatenoise.com/chocolate-and-women-part-2.

Levin, Eric. "Speak Quickly, and Carry a Big Spoon." *New Jersey Monthly*, January 12, 2010. https://njmonthly.com/articles/jersey-living/speak-quickly-and-carry-a-big-spoon/.

Martinez, Marie Elena. "Game Changer: Maricel Presilla." New Worlder. February 19, 2021. www.newworlder.com/game-changer-maricel-presilla-2/.

McKeever, Amy. "How Hoboken Chef Maricel Presilla Recovered after Hurricane Sandy." Eater. October 24, 2013. www.eater.com/2013/10/24/6348657/how-hoboken-chef-maricel-presilla-recovered-after-hurricane-sandy.

Rahmanan, Anna. "Maricel Presilla: 'I Think We're in for Other Surprises in the Future.'" HuffPost. September 14, 2020. www.huffpost.com/entry/maricel-presilla-voices-in-food_l_5f58f583c5b6b48507faa6e1.

Sandra Cisneros

Alexander, Kerri Lee. "Sandra Cisneros." National Women's History Museum. 2019. www.womenshistory.org/education-resources/biographies/sandra-cisneros.

Cisneros, Sandra. "About My Life and Work." SandraCisneros.com. Accessed May 3, 2024. www.sandracisneros.com/mylifeandwork.

Knopf Group. "Sandra Cisneros—Early Life." YouTube video, 3:14 min. March 5, 2009. www.youtube.com/watch?v=4CuRcFkH9nU.

PBS NewsHour. "Sandra Cisneros Looks Back as a Writer in Search of Home." Video, 6:21 min. October 29, 2015. www.pbs.org/video/sandra-cisneros-looks-back-as-a-writer-in-search-of-home-1453419833/.

WNYC. "Sandra Cisneros: I Hate the Iowa Writers' Workshop." YouTube video, 6:06 min. April 23, 2009. www.youtube.com/watch?v=kmEOylWMdi8.

Mari Carmen Ramírez

Alvarez Gallery. "Mari Carmen Ramirez." Accessed May 3, 2024. https://alvarezgallery.com/mari-carmen-ramirez/.

Atwood, Roger. "Remapping the Territory: Mari Carmen Ramírez and the Curating of Latin American Art." *Artnews*, December 2006. https://rogeratwood.com/article/remapping-territory-mari-carmen-ramirez-curating-latin-american-art/.

Lacayo, Richard. "25 Most Influential Hispanics in America: Mari Carmen Ramírez." *Time*, August 22, 2005. https://content.time.com/time/specials/packages/article/0,28804,2008201_2008200_2008223,00.html.

Ellen Ochoa

American Physical Society. "Ellen Ochoa." Accessed May 3, 2024. www.aps.org/careers/physicists/profiles/ochoa.cfm.

Brennan, Carol. "Ochoa, Ellen: 1958–:Astronaut." Encyclopedia.com. Updated May 18, 2018. www.encyclopedia.com/people/history/historians-miscellaneous-biographies/ellen-ochoa.

Encyclopaedia Britannica. "Ellen Ochoa." Updated May 11, 2024. www.britannica.com/biography/Ellen-Ochoa.

National Aeronautics and Space Administration. "Ellen Ochoa." Accessed May 3, 2024. www.nasa.gov/people/ellen-ochoa/.

Space Center Houston. "Astronaut Friday: Ellen Ochoa." October 4, 2019. https://spacecenter.org/astronaut-friday-ellen-ochoa/.

Rigoberta Menchú Tum

Encyclopaedia Britannica. "Rigoberta Menchú." Updated March 26, 2024. www.britannica.com/biography/Rigoberta-Menchu.

Nobel Prize, The. "Rigoberta Menchú Tum Biographical." Accessed May 11, 2024. www.nobelprize.org/prizes/peace/1992/tum/biographical/.

Welker, Glenn, comp. "Homage to/Homenaje a Rigoberta Menchú Tum: Quiche Mayan." Indigenous Peoples Literature. Updated May 31, 2019. www.indigenouspeople.net/menchu.htm.

Isabel Toledo

Cannon, Elizabeth. "Isabel Toledo." *Bomb*, July 1, 1989. https://bombmagazine.org/articles/1989/07/01/isabel-toledo/.

Chrisman-Campbell, Kimberly. "Isabel Toledo: Beyond the Michelle Obama Dress." *Atlantic*, August 28, 2019. www.theatlantic.com/entertainment/archive/2019/08/isabel-toledo-beyond-michelle-obama-dress/596950/.

Friedman, Vanessa. "Isabel Toledo Dies at 59; Designed Michelle Obama's Inaugural Outfit." *New York Times*, August 26, 2019. www.nytimes.com/2019/08/26/style/isabel-toledo-dead.html.

Penrose, Nerisha. "Designer Isabel Toledo Has Died." *Elle*, August 26, 2019. www.elle.com/culture/celebrities/a28819424/isabel-toledo/.

Thurman, Judith. "Remembering Isabel Toledo, a Designer with Few Peers." *New Yorker*, September 4, 2019. www.newyorker.com/culture/postscript/remembering-isabel-toledo-a-designer-with-few-peers.

Jean-Michel Basquiat

Artnet. "Jean-Michel Basquiat." Accessed May 3, 2024. www.artnet.com/artists/jean-michel-basquiat/.

Rosenberg, Bonnie. "Jean-Michel Basquiat." The Art Story. November 22, 2011. www.theartstory.org/artist/basquiat-jean-michel/.

Sawyer, Miranda. "The Jean-Michel Basquiat I Knew . . ." *Guardian*, September 3, 2017. www.theguardian.com/artanddesign/2017/sep/03/jean-michel-basquiat-retrospective-barbican.

Sotheby's. "Jean-Michel Basquiat." Accessed May 3, 2024. www.sothebys.com/en/artists/jean-michel-basquiat.

Wainwright, Lisa S. "Jean-Michel Basquiat." Encyclopaedia Britannica. Updated August 8, 2024. www.britannica.com/biography/Jean-Michel-Basquiat.

Mónica Ponce de León

Architect Magazine. "Monica Ponce de Leon Named a Carnegie Corp. 'Great Immigrant.'" July 1, 2020. www.architectmagazine.com/awards/monica-ponce-de-leon-named-a-carnegie-corp-great-immigrant_o.

Carnegie Corporation of New York. "Monica Ponce de Leon." Accessed May 3, 2024. www.carnegie.org/awards/honoree/monica-ponce-de-leon/.

Ponce de León, Mónica. "Mónica Ponce de León on Widening Access to Technology: 'If We Continue with the "Expertise" Model, Architecture Will Never Change.'" *Frame*, November 12, 2020. https://frameweb.com/article/monica-ponce-de-leon-on-widening-access-to-technology-if-we-continue-with-the-expertise-model-architecture-will-never-change.

SCI-Arc Media Archive. "Mónica Ponce de Léon: Speculations." YouTube video, 50:29 min. March 28, 2018. www.youtube.com/watch?v=qhrmponzeQg.

TEDx Talks. "TEDxUofM—Monica Ponce de Leon—The New Architect." YouTube video, 14:52 min. April 8, 2011. www.youtube.com/watch?v=kYdL4qXe8yM.

Máxima Acuña de Chaupe

EarthRights International. "Maxima Acuña-Atalaya v. Newmont Mining Corp." Accessed May 3, 2024. https://earthrights.org/case/maxima-acuna-atalaya-v-newmont-mining-corp/.

Gariwo. "Máxima Acuña." Accessed May 3, 2024. https://en.gariwo.net/righteous/environment-and-climate-change/maxima-acua-19563.html.

Goldman Environmental Prize, The. "Máxima Acuña." Accessed May 3, 2024. www.goldmanprize.org/recipient/maxima-acuna/.

Ruiz, Adriana. "Maxima Acuña: In Defense of the Land." The Borgen Project. November 15, 2019. https://borgenproject.org/maxima-acuna/.

Zoeller, Chezza. "Environmental Justice Hero: Máxima Acuña." One Earth. December 1, 2023. www.oneearth.org/environmental-justice-hero-maxima-acuna/.

Sylvia Poll

Brien, Taylor. "Top 9 Olympic Upsets: #8 Sylvia Poll." *Swimming World*, December 2, 2015. www.swimmingworldmagazine.com/news/swimming-world-presents-top-9-olympic-upsets-8-sylvia-poll/.

Costa Rica News. "Sylvia Poll: From Olympic Champion to Women's Empowerment Champion." January 9, 2023. https://thecostaricanews.com/sylvia-poll-from-olympic-champion-to-womens-empowerment-champion/.

Dodds, Tracy. "In the Water, Out of Sight: Costa Rican Swimmer Sylvia Poll Is Training Quietly for Olympics." *Los Angeles Times*, September 4, 1988. www.latimes.com/archives/la-xpm-1988-09-04-sp-2256-story.html.

Panam Sports. "Panam Sports Legends: Sylvia Poll." December 10, 2018. www.panamsports.org/en/news-sport/panam-sports-legends-sylvia-poll/.

Rico. "Costa Rican Olympic Medalist Sylvia Poll Highlights That She Was a Nicaraguan Immigrant and Asks for Solidarity with Costa Rica." Q Costa Rica. August 21, 2018. https://qcostarica.com/costa-rican-olympic-medalist-sylvia-poll-highlights-that-she-was-a-nicaraguan-immigrant-and-asks-for-solidarity-with-costa-rica/#google_vignette.

Berta Cáceres

Beam. "The Story of Berta Cáceres: How Her Fight for Indigenous, Environmental and Gender Rights Cost Her Her Life." May 2, 2019. https://medium.com/thebeammagazine/the-story-of-berta-caceres-how-her-fight-for-indigenous-environmental-and-gender-rights-cost-her-20245460b74d.

Goldman Environmental Prize, The. "Berta Cáceres." Accessed May 3, 2024. www.goldmanprize.org/recipient/berta-caceres/.

Shakira

Biography.com. "Shakira." Updated April 8, 2021. www.biography.com/musicians/shakira.

Encyclopaedia Britannica. "Shakira." Updated April 29, 2024. www.britannica.com/biography/shakira.

Garces, Isabella. "Before She Was a Global Superstar, Shakira Unified a Country Breaking at the Seams." *Esquire*, January 31, 2020. www.esquire.com/entertainment/music/a30719784/shakira-music-career-then-vs-now-colombia-impact/.

Abuelas de Plaza de Mayo

Abuelas de Plaza de Mayo. Home page. Accessed May 3, 2024. https://abuelas.org.ar/.

History.com. "Las Abuelas de Plaza de Mayo." Video, 2:35 min. March 8, 2019. www.history.com/topics/womens-history/las-abuelas-de-plaza-de-mayo-argentina-video.

Politi, Daniel, and Ernesto Londoño. "29 Argentines Sentenced to Life in Prison in 'Death Flights' Trial." *New York Times*, November 29, 2017. www.nytimes.com/2017/11/29/world/americas/argentina-death-flights-trial-dictatorship.html.

Retro Report. "Where Is My Grandchild?" *New York Times*. Video, 15:05 min. October 11, 2015. www.nytimes.com/video/us/100000003971186/where-is-my-grandchild.html.

Luis von Ahn

Medeiros, João. "Luis von Ahn Created the reCaptcha. Now He Wants to Help You to Learn a New Language." *Wired*, August 29, 2013. www.wired.com/story/a-machine-translator-that-speaks-to-the-crowd/.

Smale, Will. "The Man Teaching 300 Million People a New Language." BBC. January 26, 2020. www.bbc.com/news/business-51208154.

Soper, Taylor. "Inside the Mind of Duolingo CEO Luis von Ahn as $700M Language Learning Startup Eyes IPO in 2020." GeekWire. February 23, 2018. www.geekwire.com/2018/inside-mind-duolingo-ceo-luis-von-ahn-700m-language-learning-startup-preps-ipo/.

von Ahn, Luis. "Luis von Ahn." Carnegie Mellon University. Accessed May 3, 2024. www.cs.cmu.edu/~biglou/.

Victor Pineda

Bioneers. "Dr. Victor Pineda: Radical Inclusion Addresses the Vulnerabilities of Every Person." December 20, 2017. https:/bioneers.org/dr-victor-pineda-radical-inclusion-addresses-the-vulnerabilities-of-every-person-ztvz1217/.

Coltoff, Lily. "Dr. Victor Santiago Pineda Transforms Rights into Practice in Cities around the World." Disability Belongs. September 23, 2020. www.respectability.org/2020/09/victor-pineda-profile/.

Crawford, Krysten. "Alum Victor Santiago Pineda, Director of UC Berkeley's Inclusive Cities Lab, on Making the Future Accessible." Berkeley Haas. October 27, 2020. https://newsroom.haas.berkeley.edu/alum-victor-santiago-pineda-director-of-uc-berkeleys-inclusive-cities-lab-on-making-the-future-accessible/.

Heumann, Judith. "Dr. Victor Pineda and Advocacy The Heumann Perspective." YouTube video, 11:35 min. August 26, 2020. www.youtube.com/watch?v=nlFEPxPL1wQ.

Pineda, Victor, and Alice Wong. "DVP Interview: Victor Pineda and Alice Wong" (December 17, 2014). Disability Visibility Project. April 26, 2015. https://disabilityvisibilityproject.com/2015/04/26/dvp-interview-victor-pineda-and-alice-wong/.

Ruben Vives

All Things Considered. "Ruben Vives, from Undocumented Life to the Pulitzer Prize." NPR. December 13, 2014. www.npr.org/2014/12/13/369014806/ruben-vives-from-undocumented-life-to-the-pulitzer-prize.

Hernandez, Kristian. "Rubén Vives, Los Angeles Times Reporter, Awarded the Gold Medal for Public Service, the Most Prestigious of the Pulitzer Prizes." Borderzine. May 6, 2011. https://borderzine.com/2011/05/ruben-vives-los-angeles-times-reporter-awarded-the-gold-medial-for-public-service-the-most-prestigious-of-the-pulitzer-prizes/.

Rodriguez, Tomas A. "From Copy Boy to Pulitzer Prize Winner; Ruben Vives' Path to Success." Latino Reporter. September 8, 2017. http://latinoreporter.org/2017/copy-boy-pulitzer-prize-winner-ruben-vives-path-success/.

Tompkins, Al. "LA Times Public Service Pulitzer Winner Combined Traditional City Hall Beat Reporting with Innovative Digital Storytelling." Poynter. April 19, 2011. www.poynter.org/reporting-editing/2011/la-times-public-service-pulitzer-winner-combined-traditional-city-hall-beat-reporting-with-innovative-digital-storytelling/.

Carolina Contreras

Create and Cultivate. "This Founder's Curly Hair Salon Is Helping Women and Girls Love Themselves Just as They Are." June 8, 2020. www.createcultivate.com/blog/small-business-advice-carolina-contreras-miss-rizos.

Garcia, Sandra E. "At a Santo Domingo Hair Salon, Rethinking an Ideal Look." *New York Times*, December 30, 2015. www.nytimes.com/2016/01/03/travel/santo-domingo-dominican-hair-salon.html.

HipLatina. "Miss Rizos Is Encouraging Curly Haired Latinas to Take Up Space." November 1, 2018. https://hiplatina.com/carolina-contreras-miss-rizos-curly-haired-latinas/.

Leon, Ghislaine. "Meet Miss Rizos, the Woman behind One of Santo Domingo's Only Natural Hair Salons." Remezcla. December 30, 2015. https://remezcla.com/features/culture/meet-miss-rizos-the-woman-behind-santo-domingos-first-natural-hair-salon/.

Santos, Mariela. "The Afro-Latinx Movement for Natural Hair Is Happening on Instagram." Daily Dot. November 11, 2018. www.dailydot.com/irl/afro-latinx-natural-hair/.

Wit López

Heberling, Rachel. "Reclaiming Perspective—An Interview with Wit Lopez." Frontline Arts. August 12, 2020. www.frontlinearts.org/frontlineblog/2020/8/10/witlopez.

Museum for Art in Wood. "Young Artist Speaker Series: Wit López." YouTube video, 42:35 min. July 22, 2020. www.youtube.com/watch?v=aqB_nQXuAbA.

Owens, Ernest. "LGBTQ&A: Wit López." *Philadelphia*, June 23, 2017. www.phillymag.com/news/2017/06/23/lgbtqa-wit-lopez/.

Philadelphia Contemporary. "Talking Breakfast with Wit López." YouTube video, 6:50 min. December 17, 2020. www.youtube.com/watch?v=bEZo-sF3CR8.

Roach, Imani. "Wit Lopez on Breaking the Fourth Wall." Artblog. December 22, 2017. www.theartblog.org/2017/12/wit-lopez-on-breaking-the-fourth-wall/.

Jillian Mercado

Business of Fashion, The. "Jillian Mercado." Accessed May 3, 2024. www.businessoffashion.com/community/people/jillian-mercado.

Lu, Wendy. "Jillian Mercado on Being a Disabled Latina Model: 'We're Not Going Anywhere.'" HuffPost. September 16, 2019. www.huffpost.com/entry/jillian-mercado-disabled-latina-model_n_5d5aa4b1e4b0eb875f26d49d.

NowThis. "How Beyoncé and Target Model Jillian Mercado Is Normalizing Disabilities in Fashion." YouTube video, 4:05 min. July 9, 2019. www.youtube.com/watch?v=VhnW0n4FUw4.

Russo, Gianluca. "Jillian Mercado on Her Runway Debut and Fighting for the Disabled Community." *Teen Vogue*, March 9, 2020. www.teenvogue.com/story/jillian-mercado-runway-debut.

Yates, Jacqueline Laurean. "Model Jillian Mercado Dedicates Fashion Week Moment to Anyone with Disabilities Who 'Has Felt Unseen and Unheard.'" Good Morning America. February 11, 2020. www.goodmorningamerica.com/style/story/model-jillian-mercado-dedicates-fashion-week-moment-disabilitoes-68908975.

Elizabeth Acevedo

Articulate. "Elizabeth Acevedo's Literary Realizations." Video, 7:07 min. Accessed May 3, 2024. https://articulateshow.org/videos/elizabeth-acevedos-literary-realizations/.

Balbastro, Jackie. "Interview with Elizabeth Acevedo." Pine Reads Review. August 14, 2020. www.pinereadsreview.com/blog/interview-with-elizabeth-acevedo/.

Blue Flower Arts. "Elizabeth Acevedo." Accessed May 3, 2024. https://blueflowerarts.com/artist/elizabeth-acevedo/.

Burgess, Matthew. "The Braver We Become: A Conversation with Elizabeth Acevedo." *Teachers and Writers Magazine*, April 20, 2020. https://teachersandwritersmagazine.org/the-braver-we-become-an-interview-with-elizabeth-acevedo/.

Cummings, Monique-Marie. "Elizabeth Acevedo Sees Fantastical Beasts Everywhere." *Smithsonian Magazine*, May 5, 2020. www.smithsonianmag.com/smithsonian-institution/poet-and-author-elizabeth-acevedo-sees-fantastical-beasts-everywhere-180974806/.

Dior Vargas

If Me. "Get to Know Dior Vargas, Creator of the People of Color and Mental Illness Photo Project." Medium. April 15, 2019. https://medium.com/ifme/get-to-know-dior-vargas-creator-of-the-people-of-color-mental-illness-photo-project-168edeaff1bb.

Negron, Loren. "Mental Health Is the Center of It All." *Daily Evergreen*, February 28, 2020. https://dailyevergreen.com/75029/news/mental-health-is-the-center-of-it-all/.

Nunez, Vivian. "Dior Vargas Is Taking the Cultural Stigma out of Mental Illness." *Forbes*, July 26, 2016. www.forbes.com/sites/viviannunez/2016/07/26/dior-vargas-is-taking-the-cultural-stigma-out-of-mental-illness/?sh=4b129ad57504.

O'Shaughnessy, Lauren. "Bad Things Don't Always Last: An Interview with Dior Vargas." Made of Millions. Accessed May 3, 2024. www.madeofmillions.com/articles/bad-things-dont-always-last-an-interview-with-dior-vargas.

Stage, Dese'Rae L. "Dior Vargas." Live through This. September 26, 2014. https://livethroughthis.org/dior-vargas/.

Alexandria Ocasio-Cortez

Alter, Charlotte. "Inside Rep. Alexandria Ocasio-Cortez's Unlikely Rise." *Time*, March 21, 2019. https://time.com/longform/alexandria-ocasio-cortez-profile/.

Biography.com. "Alexandria Ocasio-Cortez." Updated May 13, 2021. www.biography.com/political-figures/alexandria-ocasio-cortez.

Office of Alexandria Ocasio-Cortez. "About." Accessed May 3, 2024. https://ocasio-cortez.house.gov/about.

Ruffner, Zoe. "Congresswoman Alexandria Ocasio-Cortez on Self-Love, Fighting the Power, and Her Signature Red Lip." *Vogue*, August 21, 2020. www.vogue.com/article/alexandria-ocasio-cortez-beauty-secrets.

Yalitza Aparicio

Cuarón, Alfonso. "Yalitza Aparicio." *Time*, 2019. https://time.com/collection/100-most-influential-people-2019/5567863/yalitza-aparicio/.

Luna, Diego. "Diego Luna Interviews 'Roma' Oscar Nominee Yalitza Aparicio—Exclusive." IndieWire. February 13, 2019. www.indiewire.com/awards/industry/diego-luna-roma-interview-yalitza-aparicio-1202043684/.

PBS NewsHour. "'Roma' Star Yalitza Aparicio on Balancing Acting and Activism." Video, 7:39 min. March 19, 2020. www.pbs.org/newshour/show/roma-star-yalitza-aparicio-on-balancing-acting-and-activism.

Tillman, Laura. "Yalitza Aparicio of 'Roma' and the Politics of Stardom in Mexico." *New York Times*, January 17, 2019. www.nytimes.com/2019/01/17/movies/yalitza-aparicio-roma.html.

Wellesley College. "An Evening with Yalitza Aparicio." YouTube video, 62:05 min. November 12, 2019. www.youtube.com/watch?v=r1hlcufXKsk.

Indya Moore

D'Addario, Daniel. "'Pose' Star Indya Moore Reflects on Activism and the Road Ahead." *Variety*, June 3, 2020. https://variety.com/2020/tv/features/indya-moore-pose-transgender-community-pride-1234623265/.

Mock, Janet. "Indya Moore." *Time*, 2019. https://time.com/collection/100-most-influential-people-2019/5567698/indya-moore/.

Slater, Bailey. "Indya Moore." *Wonderland*, July 20, 2020. www.wonderlandmagazine.com/2020/07/20/indya-moore-summer-2020-issue/.

Yuan, Jada. "Indya Moore Just Wants to Be Free." *Elle*, May 9, 2019. www.elle.com/culture/movies-tv/a27378298/indya-moore-transgender-pose-interview/.

Jamie Margolin

Brunner, Jim. "Seattle's Jamie Margolin Is 17 and a Climate Activist. On Wednesday She Testifies before Congress." *Seattle Times*, September 17, 2019. www.seattletimes.com/seattle-news/environment/seattles-jamie-margolin-is-17-and-a-climate-activist-on-wednesday-she-testifies-before-congress/.

Climate One. "Jamie Margolin." Accessed May 3, 2024. www.climateone.org/people/jamie-margolin.

Jarvis, Brooke. "The Teenagers at the End of the World." *New York Times*, July 21, 2020. www.nytimes.com/interactive/2020/07/21/magazine/teenage-activist-climate-change.html.

Margolin, Jamie. "Youth Activist Jamie Margolin on Climate Justice, the Election, and the Next Wave of LGBTQ Advocacy." GLAAD. October 7, 2020. https://glaad.org/jamie-margolin-election-climate-justice-lgbtq-advocacy.

Murray, Rheana. "Jamie Margolin of Zero Hour Is the Teen Climate Change Activist You Need to Know." Today. October 3, 2019. www.today.com/style/jamie-margolin-zero-hour-teen-climate-change-activist-you-need-t163503.

Jharrel Jerome

Aviles, Gwen. "Jharrel Jerome Is the First Afro-Latino and Dominican to Win an Acting Emmy." NBC News. September 23, 2019. www.nbcnews.com/news/latino/jharrel-jerome-first-afro-latino-dominican-win-emmy-n1057606.

Carey, Matthew. "'I Flipped Out': Actor Jharrel Jerome on Landing Breakthrough Role in Central Park Five Miniseries 'When They See Us.'" Deadline. June 18, 2019. https://deadline.com/2019/06/when-they-see-us-jharrel-jerome-moonlight-netflix-emmys-interview-1202629407/.

DuVernay, Ava, dir. *When They See Us*. 2019; Netflix.

Nash, Sydney. "Jharrel Jerome." ContentMode. Accessed May 3, 2024. www.contentmode.com/jharrel-jerome/.

Valentini, Valentina. "After 'When They See Us,' Jharrel Jerome Is Ready for His Next Big Challenge." Shondaland. September 17, 2019. www.shondaland.com/watch/a29072471/jharrel-jerome-emmys/.

Sophie Cruz

Define American. "Sophie Cruz at the Women's March on Washington." YouTube video, 2:58 min. January 21, 2017. www.youtube.com/watch?v=qPa464CEbuE.

Hernández, Arelis R. "Meet Sophie Cruz, 5-Year-Old Who Gave the Pope a Letter Because She Doesn't Want Her Parents Deported." *Washington Post*, September 23, 2015. www.washingtonpost.com/news/local/wp/2015/09/23/meet-the-5-year-old-who-gave-the-pope-a-letter-because-she-doesnt-want-her-parents-deported/.

Mendoza, Paola. "Free Like the Birds." Video, 10:01 min. 2016. https://vimeo.com/162181623.

Simón, Yara. "ICYMI: Youngest Immigration Activist Sophie Cruz Gave Jorge Ramos a Hell of a Pep Talk." Remezcla. March 21, 2016. https://remezcla.com/culture/sophie-cruz-despierta-america-jorge-ramos/.

······· **ABOUT THE AUTHOR** ·······

MÓNICA MANCILLAS is a musician, an educator, and an author of picture books and middle grade fiction and nonfiction. She holds a BA in anthropology from the University of California, Berkeley. Her books include *Mariana and Her Familia*, *The Worry Balloon*, *How to Speak in Spanglish*, *Sing It Like Celia*, and *Taco Tuesdays*. She lives in the United Kingdom with her much-adored daughter, husband, and dog, Annie.

······· **ABOUT THE ILLUSTRATOR** ·······

ISADORA ZEFERINO is an illustrator and a comic book artist from Rio de Janeiro, Brazil. They were featured in Taschen's *The Illustrator: 100 Best from Around the World*. They are the illustrator of the graphic novel *Mismatched* by Anne Camlin and have also created Brazilian covers for many beloved classics, including *A Wrinkle in Time*, *Matilda*, and *The Princess Diaries*. They live and work in Brazil.